Victory out of

Norman Maclean

Alpha Editions

This edition published in 2024

ISBN : 9789362920317

Design and Setting By
Alpha Editions
www.alphaedis.com
Email - info@alphaedis.com

As per information held with us this book is in Public Domain. This book is a reproduction of an important historical work. Alpha Editions uses the best technology to reproduce historical work in the same manner it was first published to preserve its original nature. Any marks or number seen are left intentionally to preserve its true form.

Contents

PREFACE ....- 1 -
NOTE ....- 2 -
CHAPTER I ....- 3 -
CHAPTER II ....- 8 -
CHAPTER III ....- 11 -
CHAPTER IV ....- 15 -
CHAPTER V ....- 19 -
CHAPTER VI ....- 27 -
CHAPTER VII ....- 33 -
CHAPTER VIII ....- 43 -
CHAPTER IX ....- 48 -
CHAPTER X ....- 51 -
CHAPTER XI ....- 58 -
CHAPTER XII ....- 62 -
CHAPTER XIII ....- 66 -

PREFACE

There is a joy in battle; but the greatest of all joys is to take some part, however humble, in the fight for the triumph of righteousness. There is a thrill such as can be found nowhere else in facing a mass of people whose prejudices and social customs are as an unscalable wall, in compelling their attention and, at last, in winning them to espouse your cause. To fight your opponent, loving him all the time, is the essence of Christianity. The excitement of betting on races or watching football matches is nothing compared to the excitement of facing an audience not knowing whether you are to be trampled on or to be applauded. Those who have fought under the banner of the King of Kings know the indefinable joy there is in it. That is why the young and the chivalrous give a swift response when the call is to a forlorn hope in the service of Christ.

And the joy of it is this, that, whatever may happen, you are bound to win. The Infinite has infinite resources. Those who array themselves against Him are up against all the forces in the universe. The fight for the Kingdom of God is the greatest in which man ever fought; it goes on ceaselessly without any discharge; the big battalions seem always on the other side; but God always wins. There never has been a fight for deliverance, a struggle for progress, but the forces of righteousness conquered at last.

This book is the third of a series. The Great Discovery portrayed the spiritual emotions of the Great War; Stand up, Ye Dead dealt with the soul of the nation in the midst of its travail; and this third book seeks to point out the way of deliverance and renewal. The malady of the world is spiritual. The fountain of healing is with God.

N. M.
EDINBURGH, *September* 1922

NOTE

Chapters I, II, III, IV, VIII, IX, XI, XII, and XIII appeared in *The Glasgow Herald*, and Chapters VI, VII, and X in *The Scotsman*. Chapter V is based on an article in *The Glasgow Herald*, but it has been rewritten.

CHAPTER I

THE ONLY HOPE

'To a large extent the working people of this country do not care any more for the doctrines of Christianity than the upper classes care for the practice of that religion.'—JOHN BRIGHT in the year 1880.

It is wonderful how quickly, when a peril is past, men forget about it and straightway compose themselves to slumbrous dreams again. It was so after the Great War; it is so already regarding the great strikes. 'Don't disturb our repose,' they as good as say; 'we have had an anxious time; do let us sleep.' But wars and strikes are only symptoms of the hidden disease; and the allaying of a symptom without the healing of the disease is of all things the most dangerous. What we must consider is the disease and set ourselves to find a remedy. Then, and then only, will the symptoms harass us no more. It was a little bald man with a straggling beard and one eye that had got a little tired of the long-continued effort to look at the other, who set me thinking. The burden of his contention was that this country and the world at large is sinking back into paganism. Though I endeavour to keep an open mind and refuse to accept opinions ready-made, however much inclined I may be to shirk the preliminary fatigue of forming opinions of my own, yet the opinions of my friend are worth recording. They are at least gropings after the truth.

I

'What is the test of a Christian?' asked the little man, trying to bring his vagrant eye to bear on me; 'if we once settle that we shall be able to judge whether this is now a Christian world. The test is not beliefs or opinions regarding the Founder of Christianity (for trifles such as that men used cheerfully to burn their fellows aforetime, thinking they were doing God service); to find the true test we must go back to the only test known to those who knew Christ. What was their test? It was this—'If any man have not the Spirit of Christ, he is none of His.' That spirit was love enduring even the Cross—love emptying itself that it might serve. Now, apply that test to our social organisation to-day. In the one city you find in one street mansions such as a Roman emperor could only desire in vain; and a few yards away a street of crowded closes and airless dugouts and fetid tenements where little children perish. Herod slaughtered a score of babies and the centuries pour the vials of infamy upon him. But this holocaust goes on, year in year out, ceaselessly. Yet the dwellers in the terraces tolerate that. The causes that produce slums and keep slums full are manifest. Yet they will not rouse themselves to remove them. Is that being a Christian? We assemble in church and recite, "I believe in God the Father," and every fact of the faith we profess condemns our callous indifference. If we realised that God is the Father of these babes, we would die to save them; yet we leave them a prey to vested interests. Is that toleration of evil compatible with Christianity?'

'You forget,' I objected, 'the law of environment. No man can live ahead of his own time—at least only the great can—and we are waking up to social duty as never before.'

'Waking up!' he exclaimed; 'we are going to sleep. A Christian should never need to waken up to facts like that. He would have them as a burden ever on his heart until they were for ever banished. He would be constantly hearing the voice of Him who said of little ones like these that it was better for those who did them wrong that a millstone were hanged round their necks and that they were cast into the midst of the sea.... If only we were Christians, endued with Christ's spirit of love, we would make an end of that at once.... We are only semi-pagans.'

II

'It isn't merely what you see outside,' went on the little man, polishing his shining poll, 'but look inside the churches themselves—any one of the hundreds in this city—and what do you find? You find the house of God given over to an unholy merchandise. Every church is parcelled out into so many square feet, and these are bought and sold as ecclesiastical allotments. Did you ever think of that gruesome traffic, and the weirdness of it? That good news of Love brooding over all, caring even for the grass and the sparrow, has now become the monopoly of the renter, while the poor are shut out. And it was at first proclaimed to the poor without money and without price, committed to the winds of Galilee.'

'Put like that,' I said, 'it is rather weird.'

'Aye,' he went on, 'and every half-year managers and deacons assemble in the houses of God to traffic in these square feet of pews. There is a story how One long ago knotted a whip of cords and drove the traffickers out of His Father's house, His eyes blazing with anger. Would He not wield the same whip on these deacons and managers, and drive them out to-day? How astonished they would be, with all the law and all the vested interest on their side ... and yet that whip!'

The little man fell silent, and his strange eye looked as if he were seeing it all. And he smiled curiously.

'Did you ever trespass on an ecclesiastical allotment?' he asked jerkily. 'No! Well, it is a thing not to be done. I once trespassed on a garden allotment out in Kelvinside, just to admire some wonderful sweet-peas, and the man who owned it found me and welcomed me like a brother, and sent me away with a radiant bunch of flowers; but an ecclesiastical allotment is another story. An old heritor once said to me that the only thing that really roused the devil in a Scotsman's heart was trespassing on his ecclesiastical allotment.'

'That only shows,' I retorted, 'how dear to a Scotsman's heart his part in the Church is.'

'That is only quibbling,' jerked out the bald man.

III

'Last Sunday evening,' went on the bald man, speaking very rapidly and walking up and down the room in his excitement, 'I went to a church situated in a mean street, surrounded by closes that each holds the population of a sparse parish. A tattered bill on the door proclaimed the traffic in seats. There seemed to be no demand. There were only eighteen present. A cheap church, with varnished pews, that could hold a thousand—and only eighteen there—old people and two or three children—none who could lay hold on life with both hands. To that handful a discouraged and hopeless preacher proclaimed the evangel of the love of God ... but his voice died in the disconsolate and empty spaces.... But when I came out, there in an open space were massed thousands of men, and the air throbbed with vitality as they listened to an orator denouncing capital and proclaiming the coming of the new day when every man could have his heart's desire—money and more money.... Eighteen at the church where the salt had lost its savour, and thousands where the chaff of worldliness was the only bread served to perishing souls.'

'But you must remember that there were some churches quite full in the city that evening,' I interjected.

'Quite so,' resumed the bald man, 'but who were they that filled them? Only the one class that has still kept its hold on the seriousness and the duty of life—the middle class—the one layer of health in the nation.'

'You forget,' I protested, 'that the other two classes have proved that they know how to die.'

He came to a sudden halt, and his tripping sentences suddenly stopped.

'Yes,' he answered, 'they know how to die; but what is the use of knowing how to die if they do not know how to live?'

IV

'What is the use of facing death,' went on the bald man, resuming his walk up and down, and pointing now and again an accusing finger, 'if death does not teach the way of life? Through death we conquered the greatest tyranny that ever threatened the world, but the enemy has really been the victor, for the spirit of the enemy has now conquered us. That spirit is the covetousness that knows no law but force. It does not matter whether the goal aimed at be the hegemony of the world or more and more of gold—the spirit is the same. And now it has seized us. There is the profiteer living on the results of other men's industry and fattening on the plunder of the public—his god is covetousness. There are the millions who are ready to march over the ruins of the Empire, careless of the sufferings of others if only they will get their demands on the world. Nobody realises the futility of gaining the world and losing the life. Eighteen in church and thousands out for their share of the world.... It is covetousness triumphant.'

The old man came to a halt and began to speak as one weighing his words. 'We are just sinking into savagery,' he went on. 'The savage knows no weapon but force—and Christianity knows no weapon but love—but we have chosen force. We have, in truth, abolished the bludgeon of force as between man and man, but pagan Rome did that. We have never learned that law must rule between class and class, as well as between man and man. We remained pagan in our jealousy and distrust as between class and class, and failed to make law supreme. We failed because we had no brotherliness, no love. If we had been Christians we would have made the law of love supreme long ago.... What a hollow mockery our actions are. Our statesmen become rhetorical over a tribunal of the nations that will make wars cease for ever, while war reigns in our own midst. Tribunals and treaties are nothing if truth be not supreme in the heart. But there is never a word about that.... We think we can raise the world to a level higher than we have attained ourselves, as if water could ever rise higher than its source.... The law of force is honest paganism, but this covering up of the world's foulness with scum—that is nauseating pharisaism. Where the spirit of love and truth is not, there peace cannot be.'

V

Whether the bald man with the one piercing and the other straying eye was right or wrong I am no great judge. But it is clear that there is something very far wrong. It is not in our country, the fairest on God's earth, that the evil lies, nor in the Empire, the greatest and richest ever reared by man. The evil is not without but within us. The only hope for us is in a regenerated spirit. And there is none who can give us that new spirit but the Carpenter of

Nazareth. He was Himself a poor working man toiling for twenty years, wielding heavy, clumsy tools as he shaped rude ploughs in a village of poor fame. He can feel for poor toiling working men; it was He who first taught brotherhood. To a generation that says, 'Let me get all I can, however much others may suffer,' He says, 'Say not so, but rather say, Let me serve all I can, however much I may suffer.' If He were here now He would be talking to men in public-houses and at the street corners and on the fringes of crowds, and He would say, 'My brothers, why excite yourselves over the world? Life is not money. Life is love and beauty and sonship with God. It is not what the hand grasps but what the eye sees and the heart feels that makes life great. If you want the fulness of life, lose it.' And to rich men He would say, 'Your riches are only yours in trust that you may serve: consecrate them or they will be taken from you.' He would have but one law for all—Love. If they but loved there could not be any more profiteering, or ca' canny, or any injustice. For love never says 'Give,' only 'Let me give.' ... But, alas! we make room for every spirit but that. For forty years we have taught the children by statute, but they have not been taught that. They have been taught figures and the records that are mainly the records of crime, and the explanations that are no explanations. We must begin again and teach our children what duty is, what the love of God and man is, what reverence is, and how there is a moral purpose working out life and death—life if men conform to it and death if they defy it. We teach everything by statute except that—the one thing needful. We teach that man is to be saved by the brain; we have forgotten that salvation is of the soul. There is but one power known among men that can turn the self-willed and self-centred life into the self-sacrificing and the God-centred life, and that power is the spirit of the Carpenter of Nazareth. If we but sought it, then it would fuse the poor fissiparous sand of our national life into the unity and potency of steel. It is our only hope.

CHAPTER II

THE SUPREME NEED

'To me through these thin cobwebs Death and Eternity sat gazing.'—
THOMAS CARLYLE.

Many eager hearts looked for the redemption of mankind to come out of Armageddon. Aceldama has been cleansed, but redemption seems to tarry. And nobody need be surprised. Out of filth and mud and horror the cleansed soul does not emerge. There was a king long ago who saw ten horrible plagues succeed each other until at last the first-born lay dead—but he was the same until the sea overwhelmed him. And man is the same in all ages. Cataclysms do not work renewal. Miracles do not regenerate. Not even the millions dead will mean a new earth or a new Britain. That new Britain of the heart's desire will only come if men and women whose souls are quickened will arise and make their world anew. The world's supreme need is not reorganisation, but a new spirit.

I

The pathos of humanity is that men are ever the victims of illusion. After Waterloo, when a conflict that waged for a quarter of a century ended, our fathers hailed the millennial dawn. But, alas! Peterloo succeeded Waterloo. The nation was seized with the passion for riches. To get rich quick the nation had to be reorganised on an industrial basis, and the people were swept out of the green of England and out of the straths and valleys of Scotland into sunless, airless cities. A population that formerly lived in cottages was now piled into barracks. In mills above ground and in mines beneath little children were set to labour. Social conditions were created that destroyed two hundred babies out of a thousand in the first year of life. These conditions still continue. The pages of the Press in these last days show how horrifying they still are. There are streets in our cities which are sacrificial altars on which the little children are offered to the social Moloch.... These things came after Waterloo. The cannon-fodder of war became the cannon-fodder of industry. The small minority that got rich quick were balanced by the vast multitude who got poor quick. And for four generations the ugly streets have presented the spectacle of files of men begging for work—begging for permission to exist! To-day the files wait for the dole. The folly and the greed have worked out the inevitable consequences. History goes on monotonously repeating itself.

II

And just as a hundred years ago men thought they were going to make a new and better world by reorganisation, so also is it to-day. On all hands the cry is reorganise. In Paris and in Glasgow it is the same. In Paris they are to save the world from all future bloodshed by a treaty. That childlike faith in treaties!—they have forgotten that treaties were unable to save even one fragment of Europe eight years ago. But this time the treaty is to be so very big that it will save. But, alas! no treaty is of value beyond the truth in the soul of its signatories—and of that there is never a word. No treaty can exorcise greed, ambition, and lust out of the heart—and it is from these wars spring. If the hearts of the nations be not changed, one more mirage will be added to the many humanity has pursued across the burning sands, strewing the barren desert with bleached bones.

In London or Glasgow or Hamilton or Fife it is the same. There also the new earth is to come through redistribution. Society will be differently organised. The voice that to-day cries, 'What is yours is mine,' will to-morrow shout victory. The day of material good will come through the maximum of pay for the minimum of work. The new order will banish all our ills. But the question emerges—How is the new order to be worked? If the new order is to bless humanity it must be guided and administered by men of truth, unselfishness, and honour. Unless there be such, then the mastery of capital will be only succeeded by the tyranny of the mob. None asks how such men are to be found. The hope of the new world lies not so much in better machinery as in better men. The men in the Cabinets adjusting the map of the world and the men in the shipyards and the mines are alike in this, that they forget that man's supreme need is regeneration and not reorganisation.

III

It is on that ultimate fact—that the supreme need of the day is a new spirit—that the Church seeks to fix the attention of the nation. The Church has only one purpose—to make God blaze forth once more before the eyes of men. In that alone lies the salvation of the future. The great host of the toilers may adopt the watchword 'Brotherhood,' but that is only half a truth. A brotherhood that knows nothing of a common fatherhood will not stand the day of strain. The Church therefore proclaims the full truth that the brotherhood of men only realises itself in the Fatherhood of God. To the nations seeking a unity by way of parchments, the Church must also proclaim that there can be only one ultimate unity for nations—the only unity that will stand all strain—the unity of the Spirit. The Church has the one message for warring nations and for warring classes: 'One is your Master, even Christ, and all ye are brethren.' The Church alone can bring home to the hearts of men that the way of honour is that of service, and the path of greatness that of sacrifice. Looking back on that long road by which humanity has marched forward even to this hour, it is strange to think how the great days on which the epochs turned have not been the days of mammon-worship or of military glory, but the days on which the Cross suddenly blazed forth in the heavens, as it did to Constantine, when the summons rang—'By this sign conquer.' It was then that men set their faces to climb upward, realising that the greatest thing a man can do with his life is to lay it down. And not by a cross blazing in heaven, but by millions of crosses round which the winds moan and sigh on earth, does God summon us to-day. It is that summons the Church would sound. By the spirit of self-sacrifice, by the law of love—by these alone can the world be saved.

IV

The remedy for every woe on earth is the one commandment—'Love one another, as I have loved you.' It is so divinely simple—perhaps that is why the generations refuse to listen. The measure of the law is its greatness—'As I have loved you.' To obey that law means—blood. It was the greatness of the sacrifice that was made and the greatness of the sacrifice demanded that stirred the hearts of men to life. 'He loved me, and gave Himself for me,' the Christian said, and with rapture in his heart he looked at others and said, 'He loved that man also, and gave Himself for him. I cannot rob or murder or leave in misery a man for whom Christ's hands were nailed to the cross.' That was what revolutionised the world long ago. It is the only way in which the world can be revolutionised to-day. If only the world can be brought to listen to the law of love, the world will become new.

CHAPTER III

IN THE SACRED NAME OF LIBERTY!

'The ranks are gathering; on the one side of men rightly informed and meaning to seek redress by lawful and honourable means only, and on the other of men capable of compassion and open to reason but with personal interests at stake so vast and with all the gear and mechanism of their arts so involved in the web of past iniquity that the best of them are helpless and the wisest blind.'—The Right Hon. C. F. G. MASTEBMAN.

It is difficult for men and women to arrive at a true estimate of their own state of mind. What others think of us is often a truer gauge than what we think of ourselves, for we can only look at ourselves through the distorting glass of self-love and self-interest. In these last days we have had a wonderful revelation of what others think of us. Our hoardings and our advertisement pages are crowded with appeals which could only appeal to a generation that had ceased to think and ceased to bear upon their hearts the woes of their fellows. In the sacred name of liberty, in the cause of brotherhood and equality, we were exhorted on every horizon to hold fast and change not. And we were, above all, to beware of fanatics! We are indeed fallen very low if this measure of our intelligence be correct.

I

In the sacred name of liberty we are exhorted to lay no sacrilegious hand on the sacred ark of our licensing system. Whatever results may ensue of perishing babes and ruined manhood we must vote No Change, for liberty is great. Moloch of old was great; so great that he demanded and got the sacrifice of a child now and then. But ' Liberty' is greater still. If it be true that in proportion to the number of licences in a district is the death-rate among the babies; if in districts crowded with public-houses there be a death-rate of something like 160 to 180 per 1000 babies in the first year of life, while in districts where public-houses are rare the death-rate is about 40 per 1000 babies in the first year of life; and if we are to vote No Change and acquiesce in that in the name of liberty, how great that idol Liberty must be! We must examine it and make sure that its feet be not of clay.

II

What is freedom? Freedom is that condition of things which enables a man to co-ordinate all his faculties for the development of what is best in him.

The best a man is capable of is the evolution of a character whose uprightness and honesty will command respect. But no sooner does a man set his face toward that goal than he finds that he can only climb towards it by sacrificing the liberty of his lower nature. The animal in man must be fettered that the spirit may grow. Only so can nobility of character be produced. It is manifest then that freedom to produce character is only achieved by sacrificing liberty. The idol Liberty is not, after all, really so great.

The best in life is not, however, developed in isolation. For we are bound up with our fellow-men in the complex organism of life. And we have no right to exercise any liberty that will mean loss or injury to our fellows. It may be beneficial to me that I should have the stimulus of alcohol; it may add colour to my drab life, and make the bores that harass me more tolerable; and I may find in it a sacramental value, as it promotes the flow of easy fellowship; but if the provision made to supply one with that stimulus means the ruin of others—the perishing of babes and the destruction of homes—then I have no right to that provision. The limit of my personal freedom is the beginning of hurt or injury to my fellow-men. It is along this great line that civilisation has evolved. Each step forward has been a restriction of liberty. Every extension of the franchise has been a restriction of the power of the classes that ruled previously; each new law a restriction of the right to do what one liked. Every great social advance has been a restriction of previous liberty. No man is free now to leave his children uneducated; no employer is free to deal as he pleases with his employed. No sooner is the child born than the law has it in its grip: within a few days the parent must register it and give a biography of its ancestors to a registrar; then it ordains that it be inoculated. At five years of age the child is deprived of liberty, for he is shut up in barracks and then made a prisoner for ten years, compelled to learn things that will never be of any value in all the after years. After he has escaped from that prison-house, there comes an interval of illusory liberty. He comes and goes as he likes after the hours of toil. Then comes an emotional crisis and he marries—and what is there left of his liberty? Every family is established on this—the restriction of liberty. The traffic in the street and the narcotic in the shop are alike in the grasp of law. From the cradle to the grave a man is surrounded with restrictions of liberty. There is no base liberty left to-day but the liberty to get drunk. In the name of freedom there must come an end to that liberty.

III

And yet the horizon glows with these placarded appeals to leave things as they are in the name of liberty. There is a true feeling behind these appeals— the feeling that above all things Scotsmen love freedom. And so they do.

There is no race under the sun that have hazarded their lives so much and so frequently for freedom as we have done. How it stirs our blood to read the words in which our ancestors in the year 1320 defied the Pope when his Holiness sided with England against King Robert Bruce. 'The wrongs which we have suffered under the tyranny of Edward are beyond description,' wrote the nobility and commonalty of Scotland in Parliament assembled, '... while a hundred of us exist we will never submit to England. We fight not for glory, wealth, or honour, but for that liberty without which no virtuous man can survive.' We know the end of that and of every fight our fathers fought for liberty. It was the moorsmen and cottars of Scotland, who defied three kingdoms, and fought on with the Bible in one hand and the sword in the other, that saved the liberties of nations. But what liberty was it they fought for? The liberty to get drunk! The liberty to establish at every street corner a centre for the spreading of disease, misery, and pauperism! Those who make such appeals surely underrate the intelligence of a generation who have not yet quite forgotten the exploits and the sacrifices of their sires. The freedom they achieved was the freedom to worship God as their consciences directed, and to develop that national character of uprightness and understanding that has been so fraught with blessing to the world. And that freedom it is left to us to carry to fruition—by developing a State that shall be free from ignorance, from degradation, from vice, from self-indulgence—in one word, from drunkenness in every form. 'He who will not give up a little temporary liberty for essential safety, deserves neither liberty nor safety,' declared Benjamin Franklin. We shall awake and establish public safety on the ruins of a false and a degrading liberty. When we shall have achieved that—then we shall be free indeed.

IV

Nothing appeals to my own heart so much as the anxiety shown by those publicists regarding my taxation. They feel so much for me, and are afraid that I shall require to pay more of an income-tax if I do not vote No Change. This care for my personal interests touches me profoundly; and the desire that the nation should drink itself into financial prosperity must affect every patriot's heart. But, again, Scotsmen can think. And no sooner do we exercise our minds than we see how fallacious all this is—and how ungrounded our fears. The greatest loss the nation siistains is the revenue from alcohol. What are the losses that are entailed by that revenue? Against it must be put the pauperism that the State has to support, and which is mainly caused by alcohol; the cost of "police and judges and prisons that are mainly required because of alcohol; the loss to the State of the lives wasted and ruined by alcohol. Strike a balance—and there is no gain to the State from the revenues of alcohol. The greatest loss the State sustains is the revenue it derives from the misery and degradation of its citizens. No State can grow rich by exploiting the misery and the vice of its own people. Were the money now wasted in this non-productive trade devoted to industry, the resultant product would pay the State over and over again for any loss from the sacrifice of alcohol. Already this is being proved in the United States. In the State of Massachusetts an increase in the taxation of theatres, soft drinks, candy, and transport not only made up for the loss from the taxes on alcohol, but realised an increase of over 500,000 dollars in the first dry year! There in America the breweries and distilleries are being converted into jam factories, boot factories, and where formerly 250 men were employed they now employ 1500 men! One such factory bears the placard:—

'Once we made booze,
Now we make shoes.'

The revenue that comes from prosperity enriches a nation; the revenue that comes from its degradation impoverishes. When we are freed from the waste and ruin wrought by alcohol—then our national revenue will nourish as never before. In a prosperous land the revenue will look after itself. Those who are so anxious lest we be overtaxed are trying to inspire us with groundless fears.

V

The most sacred thing on earth is the mother and the child. It is they who suffer and perish because of conditions that are indefensible. The little spark of grey matter behind the eyes of a little child may become a Newton, a Knox, or a Walter Scott. 'There is no wealth but life,' declared Ruskin. Every motive of patriotism and religion moves us to do everything in our power to save childhood and motherhood. There never in any land was any propaganda so cynical, so unblushing as the propaganda that for weary weeks has now screamed in our ears—'No Change.' The blood of four dread years, and then—'No Change!' The agony of the world's most awful Gethsemane, and at its end—'No Change!' ... Nothing more need be said. Only the blind could have made such appeals.

CHAPTER IV

THE GREATEST OF TYRANNIES

The deadliest foe of humanity is the deadening power of custom. What we have seen from our earliest days has no power to stir our conscience or kindle the fire of indignation. It may be the case that when Lot went down to Sodom he was at first 'vexed with the filthy conversation of the wicked.' But he did not continue vexed very long. He got to like it. At last he sat at the gates of that city with great enjoyment. As he sank into the mire he became unconscious of the slough. Otherwise he would never have returned to it. When the great war of the five kings against four reached its consummation, and Lot was a prisoner going north with a halter round his neck, he often groaned, 'If I ever get out of this I'll never look near that filthy Sodom again.' Like a bolt from the blue came deliverance and victory and spoils—and back he went to Sodom and its filthy conversations as before. It is such a wonderfully modern story. In every age men get so accustomed to the filth that it no longer seems filth. The mud of their daily habit becomes their gold.

I

When we look back on the long road by which humanity has travelled and read of the things men once did in cold blood, we wonder how they could ever have had the heart to do them. The answer is—custom. To us it is incredible that men should once have trafficked in human flesh and blood. And yet to our forefathers of even recent years it seemed the most natural thing. Were there not slaves from the beginning, and naturally there would be unto the end! The captains of the slave ships would assemble their crews in their cabins for prayer meetings while the holds of their ships were filled with men and women dying in these gehennas! So far from experiencing any twinges of conscience, these slave captains regarded themselves as benefactors of humanity. Sir John Hawkins was not alone in priding himself on the fact that he brought so many of the heathen of Africa into Christian lands, where they might hear the Gospel. It is not so long ago when children of six years worked in factories from five in the morning to nine at night. We who play with our babes and build our brick castles in Spain while they shout for joy—think of it! What hearts they must have had—these fathers of ours—who took the babes by their thousands and harnessed them to the car of their juggernaut! And yet they were not any different from us. They were only blinded by custom.... Whoever has wandered over the hills of his native land will remember the leap of the heart when he has suddenly seen some fair valley open up before his amazed eyes. He can hear the song of the river that waters it, he sees the clouds playing on the slopes, his awestruck lips murmur with the great artist as he looked on Glen Feshie, 'Lord God Almighty!' But no human dwelling is there, only heaps of stones where the homesteads once stood; only the bleating of sheep where children once shouted at play. What became of the people? They were driven out. The will of one man or one woman drove the population of a parish into the Cowcaddens of Glasgow or exiled them beyond the seas. And the Church of Christ looked on silent. And the men who made the countryside waste prided themselves on the fact that they set the people, whom they drove forth, on the way of fortune! How could men do deeds like these? How could the Church be silent in the face of them? Again it was just custom. The ears had got so accustomed to phrases such as the 'sacredness of property,' the 'right of a man to do what he liked with his own,' that the heart forgot the sacredness of the Gospel and the rights of the people in the land of their birth. It is time we stopped mouthing about the cannon-fodder of war, and began to speak about the cannon-fodder of custom.

II

If poor, blundering, pitiful humanity had not been blinded by custom to the folly of war, it would have made an end of war long ago. But all the days of youth humanity has shut into dreary barracks, learning all sorts of foolish things. And the history it learns is just the history of war after war! At fourteen the centuries seem to a boy but a river of blood. He deems it an inevitable weapon in the progress of the world—this ceaseless killing! It is custom alone that prevents humanity from making an end of that horror. And strikes are only war in another form—the bludgeon of force! Kaiserism is not dead. World dominion for me or destruction for you has its counterpart in two shillings for me or ruin for you. The spirit is the same. If custom had not deadened us to the meaning of war and strike, we would shrink back in horror at the very sound of the words. But, instead of that, ere humanity has recovered from the woe of the one, we are plunged into the woes of the other.... It sounds a respectable sort of word! And the right of a man to stop working seems elementary—for we are not slaves. But humanity has learned there is a higher word than rights—and that is duty. We owe service to our brethren. We can pay too high a price for two shillings more a day if they mean starving women and perishing children. Life is more than livelihood; and if the endeavour to better livelihood means the destruction of life, then it is condemned. And that is what it means. Europe is perishing. Vienna is dying. All over the world Rachel is weeping for her children. What Europe needs is coal and raw materials, that it may have wherewith to buy food. And we go on strike. And ships can no longer carry food or cotton; and Europe will starve ... starving is a good discipline and I shouldn't mind ... but, God! the little children ... the babies.... 'Strike,' we shout, finding it easy through long custom. But our striking is only completing the work that Kaiserism began. And the little graves are dug faster and faster; and you can hear the falling of tears like soft rain.... What savages we are, unable through any disciple to learn that the world can only be saved by submitting to law and by ceasing to wield the bludgeon of force.... When one thinks of the poor suffering, quarrelling, dying slaves of custom; when one sees the world in one blinding flash convulsed in the death throes—Oh, God! if only there came a gale from Heaven—a sudden, rushing wind. Only that could save a world blinded like this.

III

You may imagine that I am exaggerating the power of this tyrant of whose despotism you are unconscious. But you have only to think and you will at once recognise that my words are but the words of soberness. Use your eyes as if for the first time—and what a world this is that surrounds us! I read the other day a paragraph in the morning paper that made my blood cold. A discharged soldier got his gratuity and spent his day in jollity. He came home at night and, in the presence of his children, trampled his wife to death, and not his wife only, but the unborn child—and in the presence of his children. That, in the most cultured city in Bible-loving and Christian Scotland. And every day the tale is much the same. Little children are perishing, mothers are broken-hearted, and the streets are strewn with human wreckage. The casualties of war pale in significance before the casualties of peace! But this does not move us: we are accustomed to it. These crowded, reeking public-houses, thirty to the half-mile, battening on the misery of the poor—we have seen them from our youth and they move us not. How many in our Circuses and Terraces and Places will even trouble themselves to so much as vote for the deliverance of their fellow-citizens? Very few in these particular places, if I mistake not. For they cannot shake themselves loose from the yoke of custom.

IV

And this same tyrant blinds us to the goal to which we are hastening. The last great proof of the power of custom is that when nations and empires were perishing they never knew they were perishing. Men were so accustomed to the riches and greatness and security of the Roman empire, that even when it was tottering to its fall they never realised that it was doomed. All nations have gone the one road. They have abolished God or the gods! They have cast duty to the winds; they have given themselves to Mammon and to pleasure; and they perished—but they never knew that the world that seemed to them so secure was passing away. And unless there comes a change—a mighty gale from Heaven—then this world we know must perish. Custom alone blinds us to the fact, plain to the open eye. Scotland cannot feed her people but for a few weeks in the year. For the rest they must be fed by the food brought from overseas by the fruits of our industries. If these industries fail ... we perish. The Clyde will no longer hum with the throbbing engines or great ships come with food.... And every strike, every stoppage of labour, is but a step towards the abyss.... But probably that is what God means. He makes the wrath of men to praise Him—He will use hunger as the instrument wherewith to scatter the great Scottish race broadcast over the world, to people the mighty plains of Canada and the wastes of Australasia. A great silence will fall over the plain of central Scotland. The most hideous of all the workings of man will be beautified when the lichen grows over the crumbling ruins. The mavis will sing in the thorn-tree, dewy with fragrance, where Motherwell now stands ... or Anderston. That may be the hidden purpose of our follies and our crimes. This, at least, is sure, that if we cannot shake ourselves loose from the grip of custom—custom will be our destruction.

CHAPTER V

THE LAST DELIVERANCE

Every great social advance made by men in the past has been made under the pressure of public opinion. That public opinion was created by a free and an unfettered Press. The grim fact that we are now faced with is that the day of the free Press is over. Syndicates of capitalists control the Press of the country, and newspapers whose circulation approaches a couple of millions create the opinion their owners desire. The duty of the newspaper is to record facts, and communicate to the people the correct data on which public opinion can be based. If the Press purposely suppresses what is true, lends itself to the colouring of the records so that the false seems to be the true and the true false, then it becomes the greatest public peril. A generation that is doped with doctored news can scarcely arrive at the truth. The newspapers are supplied free by the bureaux of the interested with news that serve their purpose. Thus it comes that the machinery for creating public opinion is largely in the hands of those whose purpose is that public opinion shall not destroy or lessen their profits. There are noble exceptions; but, taking it as a whole, the syndicated Press of this country is no longer a mirror of the truth.

I

In the United States of America and in Canada there are one hundred and twenty millions who speak our language, whose religion is also ours, who are the most intelligent and hard-headed people on the face of the earth, yet if one were to believe what the Press of this country says, one would be driven to the conclusion that they are poor foolish idealists who have said farewell to their senses. And that because the Press serves the public with doctored news. One day we are told how a hundred thousand New Yorkers are to march in procession through the streets demanding the return of their alcoholic drinks. The columns are full of the preparations for the greatest uprising of the oppressed and parched citizens. The great day comes and the procession is a fiasco. But the syndicated Press omit to record that only a miserable handful paraded the streets, the offscourings of the city's purlieus, amid the derision of the onlookers. We are later informed under great headlines that the American Medical Association or some such society has called for the annulling of the Prohibition Law. We feel that the climate is bound to become wet again, for the doctors demand it. But we soon learn that this particular association of doctors is a mere fragment of a noble profession—a fragment separate from the American Association which corresponds to the British Medical Association. But the syndicated Press does not record that fact. The Press that distorts events after that manner can only flourish among a generation that desires not the truth.

II

There is nothing more to be desired than that the people of Great Britain should acquaint themselves with the facts regarding the greatest social advance ever made by humanity in a generation. Can it be the case that the millions of America committed an act of social folly when they outlawed the liquor traffic and closed the saloons, and that, awakening from their dream, they are to restore the traffic in alcohol and the saloon once more? That is the impression that a spoon-fed Press seeks to create. Can it be true?

To answer that question we must ascertain first whether the prohibition of the sale and manufacture of alcohol in the States was an act of panic legislation, the result of a snap vote, the effect of a passing enthusiasm or a fanaticism that was triumphant for a moment? If it be of that order, then it may be expected to be cast aside by a wearied and disillusioned people. But the movement that prohibited alcohol across the Atlantic has the toil and sacrifice and devotion of three generations behind it. It is not a thing of yesterday. As far back as 1834 the selling of liquor to Indians was forbidden by law. Seventy-six years ago (in 1846) the first Prohibition Law was enacted in the State of Maine. Fifty-seven years ago the Presbyterian General Assembly excluded liquor distillers and liquor sellers from the membership of the Church. In 1873 the Women's Temperance Crusade movement was inaugurated—a movement whose ideal was to make the United States safe for women and children by the suppression of the saloon. In 1893 the Anti-Saloon League was formed—an organisation that brought the various societies into unity and fused them into the strength of steel. There were long years of work in school and of teaching in the churches ere on the 18th December 1917 the Amendment in favour of Prohibition passed the Legislative Assemblies at Washington. Having passed the House of Representatives and the Senate, it had to be ratified by a majority of the various States. The States had seven years in which to ratify; but within one year and two months forty-five States, with a population of over one hundred millions, ratified the Amendment. Only three out of the forty-eight States failed to ratify. On the 29th January, it being certified that three-fourths of the States had ratified as the Constitution requires, the 18th Amendment to the Constitution of the United States, prohibiting alcohol, became law. And on that night the leaders of the movement held a service of thanksgiving in Washington, and when the hour struck ushering in the first day of the new era, Mr. W. J. Bryan began his address by reading the words: 'They are dead that sought the young child's life.' An Amendment to a National Constitution which has the generations behind it is not one to be repealed. To repeal it requires now a majority of three-fourths of the States! The one great fact to remember, is that by local option two thousand two hundred and thirty-five counties in the United States had made an end of the liquor traffic in their areas before Prohibition became the national law, and that there were only three hundred and five counties in all the States which had not declared themselves dry before Prohibition became the law. If anything be certain under the sun it is that Prohibition is the settled and unalterable policy of the United States of America. During a visit of three months, and after inquiries in several cities, I never met a single person who wanted the saloon again reopened in the States. Whatever criticism might be made, there was among everybody only one sentiment regarding the saloon—and that was thankfulness that it was closed for ever.

III

There are, however, those who desire the Volstead law defining alcohol amended so that the sale of beer and light wines may be permitted in restaurants with meals. To us that seems reasonable; but there is no chance of such a policy being adopted. The reason is that these experiments have already been made in the States and have been found unworkable and unsatisfactory. The settled policy of the reformers in the States is to seal up the sources of drunkenness. Every drunkard began as a moderate drinker; and the evil has to be stayed at its source. Mr. Bryan described the process dramatically: 'The moderate drinker says every man should stop when he has had enough. But the difficulty is to know when one has had enough, for enough is a horizon that recedes as one approaches it. A frail brother was advised by a friend to drink a glass of sarsaparilla when he had had enough. "That's right," was the reply, "but when I have had enough I cannot say sarsaparilla!"' The prevailing opinion among the Church and social leaders is that the liquor trade as it was conducted in America could not be mended, and that it had to be ended. And it was ended. Having been ended, there is no possibility of its being amended!

IV

It is one thing to legislate and another to make that legislation effective. We know that by experience in this country. It took long years to make the laws against smuggling operative in this country; and it was only after Queen Victoria's accession that the laws abolishing slavery in the British Empire, passed in a previous reign, were made operative. In the States the stage of legislation regarding alcohol is past, and the stage of making the legislation effective has come. The difficulty of making Prohibition operative is great, but the difficulty is being steadily overcome. No law that ever was made has been fully successful: otherwise there would be no theft and no murder in a perfect world. In one State—Detroit—it is said that five thousand automobiles are stolen every year, but nobody ever suggested that the commandment forbidding theft should be repealed in Detroit. There are more murders in New York in any one year than in the whole of Ireland in its most distressful year, but nobody suggests that the commandment against murder should be repealed in New York. That a law is broken is no argument for its repeal. And notwithstanding all the smuggling there is no doubt but that the Prohibition Law is obeyed by 99 per cent. of the American people. 'In Nebraska there are several times as many men in the penitentiary for stealing automobiles as there are for violating the liquor laws.' The persons who are convicted for breaking the law are the aliens newly come to the country—Italians, Poles, Irish, Spaniards. A native-born American scarcely ever is found among the breakers of the Prohibition Law, and very seldom a Scotsman. But the newspapers themselves are the proof of this. If the disregard of Prohibition were the general thing, the newspapers would cease to record it; for according to the Press news is the exceptional. To walk to business every day is commonplace and receives no record; but to be run down in the traffic and break a limb is news. That receives its paragraph. It is the exceptional that receives the big headlines. And the big headlines about smuggling across the Canadian border and from the Bahama Islands or about wood alcohol are the proof that these things are exceptional. Otherwise they would not be news. That ethical passion which passed the 18th Amendment is now being diverted to its enforcement. The traffic across the Canadian border is being stopped, for Canada is now going dry. The traffic from the Bahamas under the British flag is being dealt with. 'We shall move heaven and earth to make Prohibition effective,' said the orator. 'You had better move the Bahamas,' came the reply. It would be a disaster if the false impression created in this country by the syndicated Press regarding the working of Prohibition in the States were to lead those in authority to imagine that the people of the States will regard with no indignation the British flag being used for the flouting of the laws and of the Constitution of the United States. It is impossible that that can go on. Everywhere in the States the organisation for making Prohibition effective is being tightened up. In social reform the citizens of the States are determined to lead the world. I for one am convinced that they will not be turned from their chosen path or deflected from their goal by bootleggers or by Jewish syndicates. Whoever will judge of the condition of the States regarding Prohibition from the newspapers in New York will find themselves misled. 'In New York,' says *The World*, 'it will be necessary to install three enforcement agents to a family, so that they can stand in three eight-hour shifts, or hire the entire population of the city as special enforcement agents and set every man to watch himself.' That is the sort of piffle that is supplied gratis to the newspapers in this country. What is forgotten is the fact that the millions of homes where the fathers and mothers live and toil, who have carried the law, say nothing. Their voice is not heard in their Press. And they have not weakened in their resolution that their country shall be a country where children shall grow up untempted and where monopolies shall no longer be free to fill the jails and the poorhouses. No amount of jibes can alter the fact that there has been no ethical revolution in the history of the world comparable to that passion for righteousness which passed the 18th Amendment and which is now determined to enforce it. 'Our parents,' said a wet orator lately, 'taught us to lay up something for a rainy day: how much nicer if they had only taught us to lay up something for a dry one.' The American will make any number of jokes about his climate, but his determination is unalterable that it shall be dry. There has been no great moral advance made by humanity in these last centuries which has been unable to hold its ground. Whatever dust may be thrown in their eyes, the people of this country may be certain that there will be no repeal. When the choice is 'Repeal' or 'Enforce,' the American chooses unhesitatingly. 'Enforce' becomes his watchword.

V

Though in the Western States full enforcement of the Prohibition Law has not been effected so far, yet the beneficial effects of the closing of the saloons are so many and great, that he who runs may read. There were four millions idle in the States at the time when I was there, but the nation was going through the greatest industrial crisis in its history with perfect calm, and without suffering the pangs of destitution, because workmen no longer wasted their money in the saloons. Here in Britain the idle have been pauperised by doles from the public exchequer; in the United States there have been no doles. The nation can thus come through a crisis of unemployment without half its number becoming a charge on the remainder. That is possible because the sources of waste are sealed up. Statistics amply prove that drunkenness is rapidly disappearing. The Salvation Army ceased its rescue work among the drunkards in New York because there were no more drunkards to be rescued. In Pittsburg I found the jail well-nigh empty and the poorhouse without sufficient inmates to keep it clean. It is the same everywhere. One great employer of labour, whose opinion I asked, said: 'Prohibition has given us a good Monday in our factory.' That was the most terse and effective testimony to Prohibition that I heard. There is no broken time owing to drunkenness. Industrial efficiency has been increased 20 per cent. One man who had an interest in a big hotel told me that the profits from soft drinks (non-alcoholic) were last year double the profit they used to make by the sale of alcohol. Hotels never had such a time of prosperity as they have had lately. The reason is that men can bring their wives and children to stay at the hotels with perfect safety. The proprietor of the biggest hotel in a city where I stayed told me that he was glad to be rid of the bar and that he would never have it back on any account. A Canadian-Scot who has prospered greatly told me how he became a Prohibitionist. 'I am interested in a mine in the north,' said he, 'and I went to visit it. I saw the men wasting their substance and their lives in the saloons—lying around drugged, with their pockets empty. It was shocking. I used to give $500 to fight Prohibition. When the wet agent came to my office after that for my subscription, I said: "Get out! I'll give $500 a year in the future to make an end of all saloons!" It is thus the movement spreads. The moderate drinker is as determined as the Rechabites that the saloon shall never open its door again—and it never will. One of the oddest testimonies in behalf of the success of the new law was this saying: 'In Detroit there has been a falling off in the taxi-cab trade.' The inference is that everybody can walk home now. 'We saw,' says Mr. Harold Spender, 'only a single drunken man in America for three weeks, and then he was a politician going to Washington.' In a period of three months I saw none. Though this reform has been in operation for so short a time, it has already effected the greatest miracle in modern history. It has healed the sick by the hundred thousand and it has raised the dead.

VI

The readers of the commercialised Press when they scan the inspired articles regarding America's social uprising have only to use their common-sense to realise that they are being served up falsehoods. They have only to think what a mighty change for the betterment of humanity has been wrought in the great cities where alcohol no longer seeks and lies in wait for the unwary at every street corner. Instead of liquor seeking him, the drouth must now seek the liquor—and the search is a toilsome one in a dry and parched land. What a deliverance that must be for the weak-willed when the State no longer, by licensed premises every few yards in the crowded streets, tempts them to take the road to pauperism and destruction. They have only to think of the lives of rich and poor whom they themselves knew, that have made shipwreck on these rocks and shoals, and think what a deliverance has come to the nation that no longer, with the marshalled host of its liquor sellers, seeks to enslave and destroy its citizens. They have only to look at the city of their habitation and ask themselves why it is that so many hundred thousand of their fellow-citizens live under conditions that mean unspeakable misery. Why are families doomed to one-roomed houses? why are children reared under conditions that mean their being damned before they are born? The answer is—Alcohol! In proportion to the number of public-houses in any district is the misery of the housing conditions. You have but to scratch the surface of human misery anywhere in our cities and you find the turgid stream of alcohol. Let the reader of the subsidised Press ask himself why all the money spent on clearing and cleaning slums has wrought no result? It is that alcohol creates new slums faster than the old are cleared away. Let him ask why all the money spent in mission work, in philanthropic work, in rescue work, has not diminished the mass of human misery; and the answer is—Alcohol! Let him think of the money now wasted by the workers in the reeking public-houses being used to clothe and feed and house the children—and what wonderful cities we would have and what a new race we would become. And all that has been done in the United States and in Canada. 'Our great claim as Prohibitionists,' said Admiral Sims, 'is that it has shut up the schools of future drunkards, the saloons and the clubs. We have saved the rising generation.' No amount of misrepresentations can alter facts. The Americans are not fools. They know their own business. 'In every community,' said President Harding recently, 'men and women have had an opportunity to know what Prohibition means. They know that debts are more promptly paid, that men take home the wages that once were wasted in saloons, that families are better clothed and fed, and more money finds its way into the savings bank. In another generation I believe that liquor will have disappeared, not merely from our politics, but from our memories.'

VII

Great Britain led the world in the deliverance of humanity from the degradation of slavery; the United States and Canada are leading the world in the still greater deliverance of humanity from the degradation of alcohol. Out of the West cometh the world's salvation. America, that is for ever singing of itself as the 'sweet land of liberty,' is now the seat of the greatest experiment in personal coercion that the world has known. And that is because the American has freed his mind from cant. He has replaced the conception of liberty as liberty to do as we like by the conception of liberty which is the liberation of large masses of the community from thraldom to their base appetites and from the oppression of grafters and profiteers. The main cause of that deliverance was the awakened conscience of the people. When the power to veto licences was placed in the hands of the people, the citizens became conscious of the fact that when they voted for a licence they were just as much partners in the saloon as if they furnished the liquor and sold it standing behind the bar. When they considered that the poisoning of the poor by alcohol was a road to wealth, when they traced the misery and ruin that afflicted the community to the saloons, they felt that they could not any longer be sharers in the traffic nor incur responsibility for it. It was the

Churches of the land that wakened the conscience of the people. It was better that any community perish rather than that they should offend one of the little ones for which Christ died.... What we need is that the conscience of the community should be wakened in the same manner. The Church of Christ alone can sound the trumpet that wakens from the slumber of torpor. But the Church seems more concerned about dealing out soothing syrup to its soporific members than about wakening the dead. The spectacle of bishops denouncing Prohibition in the name of Freedom; of representative Church Councils refusing to recommend the cause of No-Licence; of congregations being narcotised to the slaughter of the innocents that goes on ceaselessly all around them—the victims of Bacchus laid for ever on his altar—while the preacher proclaims peace, peace, where there is no peace, and expounds an evangel of sweetness and light while the people are perishing—all that may well make angels weep. But the Churches are wakening. The founder of Christianity prayed, 'Lead us not into temptation,' and Christians cannot for ever acquiesce in the State tempting its own children to their destruction. Just as we look back and marvel how any Christian could ever defend slavery, so fifty years hence, when the liquor traffic will have become a memory, men will marvel how Christians could ever have defended the Liquor Trade and looked on, silent, while it swept the young and the strong to doom.

CHAPTER VI

THE PERIL OF THE CROWD

The history of humanity is in large measure the history of its own illusions. It has always been towards the mirage that men have tramped with bleeding feet, only to strew the desert with bleached bones. One great illusion has been that the golden age would come when the world's autocracies gave place at last to democracy, and the will of the multitude became law. It has come; democracy now wields the world's sceptre. But alas! the golden age tarries, and the wistful doubt arises whether the greatest peril confronting humanity may not be just that—the sceptre in the hand of the unregenerate crowd.

I

For what we have to remember is that the crowd is by its very nature and spirit capable of crimes such as the individual autocrat would shrink from in horror. You may think that fantastic, and imagine that a crowd consists, after all, of so many individuals, and that the spirit of the crowd can only be the aggregate of the individuals comprising it. But such a view is mistaken. The corporate spirit of the crowd is not that of the units composing it. The best illustration of this is the sudden reeling back into the jungle of a crowd when a panic seizes them. Let the cry 'Fire' be raised in a crowded building, and though the separate individuals be of the gentlest and most considerate, yet instantly the crowd becomes dæmonic, a wrestling, writhing, struggling mass trampling the weak under foot, with no thought but self-preservation.

There are various explanations. One is the law of sympathy, by which an emotion is intensified in being shared. At the first cry of peril a wave of fear passes through the crowd; and as each looks at the faces around him he sees fear in every eye. The emotion suddenly unloosed is like a river whose source is amid the silent hills, that gathers in its course a thousand rills, until at last it sweeps in mighty floods everything before it. Before the flood of terror generated by the crowd all the decencies of civilisation vanish, and man becomes once more the animal with but the one instinct—to fight for one's life. And it is the same with anger. Let a skilled orator set himself to rouse the passion of a crowd, and he will soon generate a spirit that utterly obliterates the individual. Let him depict the wrongs they suffer, and anger sweeps through the multitude, bending them to the spirit of the orator as the corn field bends before the wind. Though as individuals they may tremble in their shoes before their wives, now, fused by rhetoric into one glowing mass, they are ready to loot a city, pull down a Bastille, and level an absolutist throne with the dust. But the great explanation of the spirit of the crowd as distinct from the individual is that in the surge of contagious emotion generated by the crowd the sense of personal identity is lost. Each only lives in the crowd. And with the loss of identity comes the loss of personal responsibility. I no longer stand alone to be judged for my acts; it is the crowd who will be judged. The brake of personal responsibility suddenly snaps. It is thus that a crowd will commit a crime that the individual afterwards remembers with horror. Only a crowd could have said: 'His blood be on us and on our children.'

In these last years the horrors that struck a chill into the heart of the world were committed by the crowd. Suddenly in a Belgian village the cry was raised, 'We are being sniped.' Instantly the soldiers were swept by one emotion, and there rose the cry for vengeance. Then the Mayor and the priest and a handful of village notables would be gathered and shot. It was the rage and panic of a crowd seeking its own safety through brutality.

It is plain, then, that the spirit of the crowd is something far other than that of the individual, and is capable of the greatest crimes. It was the crowd that compelled Socrates to drink the hemlock; it was the crowd that overbore that poor vacillating weakling, Pilate, with their monotonous chant, 'Crucify, Crucify'; it has always been the crowd that has turned the sanctuaries into the nesting-places of owls and bats; and the rock on which humanity may make shipwreck at last is just this—the crowd. The millions of the dead have made the world safe for democracy: the appalling question now is—Who will make democracy safe for the world?

II

It is, however, only when the crowd is organised that the crowd becomes a real menace. The horrors of war are unspeakable just because they are the horrors committed by the crowd perfectly organised. A crowd that has met for no purpose, and is a mere fortuitous concourse of atoms, can do neither good nor harm. In proportion to its organisation is the peril of the crowd. The power of the crowd that committed the greatest crime in the history of the world lay in the fact that it was perfectly organised. It was there in that chilly morning with only one purpose, to cry, 'Crucify, Crucify.' Across all the mists of the centuries we can see the organisers at work moving among the crowd. They whisper to one group: 'He struck you in your property, overturning the tables of your barter; if he lives you are ruined'; and to the other: 'Remember his blasphemies: what he called himself.' ... And in the trail of the organisers arose with intenser volume the cry, 'Crucify, Crucify.' It was the organised crowd that nailed the Son of Man to the cross.

The fact that confronts us to-day is that the crowd is at last perfectly organised; so perfectly organised that all the industry and transport of three kingdoms can be stopped by the flash of an electric wire. The crowd knows what it wants, and it has organised itself to get it. But the crowd to-day is not an isolated handful such as that of old in Athens or Jerusalem. The crowd is now world-wide and international. What is shouted on the banks of the Volga in the morning, at noon is shouted on the Clyde, and at the setting of the sun in New York. For the cable and the telephone and the wireless have woven humanity into one web. From the rising to the setting of the sun, slowly but steadily on the forge the international crowd is being hammered into the unity of steel.

In the old days the crowd had to storm their way into the presence of their Pilates before they could cry 'Crucify.' But to-day the organised, supernational crowd has changed all that. Now the crowd can make itself heard across half the world. It assembles on the banks of the Ganges and formulates its demands. The Turk must stay at Constantinople! If not, well, there will be trouble. There in London or Paris or Washington the modern Pilate receives his message. The cry of the crowd hums in his ears across five thousand miles. 'What shall I do with the bleeding and persecuted?' asks he. 'What is that to us?' answers the crowd on the Ganges. And expediency gains the day as it did in Jerusalem.... And fifteen thousand crosses arise with their bleeding, agonising victims in Anatolia.... The governors of this world have had but one rule in all the ages. Instead of fixing their eyes on the stars they have gazed at the streets and have listened to the crowd.... And the organised crowd can to-day make itself heard round all the world as it cries, 'Crucify, Crucify.'

III

There is to-day one other added element in the peril of the crowd, and that is the removal of the forces that formerly restrained and curbed. The witness of history is that only one spirit can stand up against and cast out the spirit of the crowd, and that is the spirit of religion. I am not speaking of Christianity merely, but of religion in its generic sense. There was only one force in Jerusalem on Good Friday stronger than the thirst for blood, and that was the feeling that they, the crowd, must not defile themselves ceremonially. Only one power, religion alone, can cut the claws of the tiger in man.... In the midst of the darkest deeds the thought of God's judgment-seat has ever and again pulled humanity up.

But it is gone now—that sense of the Unseen Assize. Two generations ago the international crowd of the learned (for crowds are of many kinds), having discovered they could explain some processes, took it for granted that nobody initiated these processes. With great congratulations on the delivery of humanity from superstition, they bowed the Creator out of His universe. In so doing they thought they were ushering in a new world, where man would find deliverance from all ill through the illumined brain.... Alas! for human hopes. The learned have now gone back to the old truth—that this world is organised spirit. But the sad thing is that though it is easy to bamboozle the crowd, yet, once they are bamboozled, it passes the wit of man to debamboozle them again. The scientific crowd bowed God out a generation ago; but to bow Him in again is beyond them. And the spirit of the crowd is left to-day without curb or chain from Siberia to Cork.

IV

There are few sadder thoughts than this—to think how the Church has thrown away the power that once it knew how to use, the mesmeric instinct of the crowd. 'In our State,' said an American, 'the devil is fighting hard against the Church!' 'Ah! in Montana it is different,' was the reply; 'there with us, the devil is running the Church.' It would look as if it were even so. Wherever there was a crowd waiting anywhere on the ministry of the Gospel, the devil set himself to break up that crowd. He did it in ways most skilful. Had his true personality appeared, he would instantly have been cast forth. It was therefore apparelled as an angel of light that he set about the work. He never failed to mouth high-sounding phrases. His favourite watchword was principle. It did not matter much what the principle was if only thereby the crowd could be broken up. In the beginning of the seventeenth century the evangel of Jesus, that was committed to the winds of Galilee and to a handful of peasants, was intellectualised into a massive system of propositions that was to be for all time the test of orthodoxy. One might smile if the fountain of tears lay not here. That religion, which is like the wind blowing where it listeth, was caught at last, and embodied in legal enactments and formulas—sheltered behind statistics! Whoever heard of wind blowing through legal documents? Build shelters and there is no more wind! Yet these legal documents became the test of that religion which is life and which is love. If any doubt was expressed about the use of shelters when men needed the fresh breeze from heaven—then the devil appeared and said that to abide by the shelter was a principle. Nobody must touch or change that structure. If that be done, then those who were loyal must separate. By a discreet use of the principle of loyalty to confessions the devil broke up crowd after crowd of worshipping Christians. There was nothing that he could not use for that purpose. The doubt arose whether the all-loving Father could really send babes to everlasting torments or decree that the vast majority of mankind be tortured, for ever and ever. That was used to break up the Church. A hymn, a paraphrase, the form of a prayer, the posture at worship, a vestment—anything, everything, was good enough for the devil's purpose. By these he achieved his ends. The crowd was no longer to be found in one sanctuary. Here, where I write, in the days of my boyhood the folk assembled in the open air for their great Christian festival on the second Sunday of August. It was a moving spectacle to see a couple of thousand people in the hearing of the sea, with the hills brooding over them, raise a psalm to heaven. But that crowd has been broken up into four fragments. There is no longer a crowd. The devil has secured its overthrow. On the wave of an emotion generated by a thousand hearts no soul shall again be wafted heavenward in that green place. For the devil has seen to it that the thousand hearts shall be no longer there.

V

There is a hopeful side to all this if only Christians will learn wisdom. Instead of allowing the devil to break up congregations into fragments, as he has done for a hundred years, what the Church must do now is to provide the crowd which will exercise the powerful attraction of the herd-instinct on the side of righteousness. The spectacle presented in a poor and crowded district of a great city by competing missions—Primitives, Wesleyans, Presbyterians, Catholics, Salvation Army, and so on—each weak and ineffective—is heart-breaking. There are so many of them that there can be a crowd at none of them. The day of home-mission activities as now conducted is at an end.... At Pittsburg I was taken to a meeting in a great auditorium, seated for 8000 people, where Gipsy Smith was carrying on a mission. The place was crowded. There was a massed choir of a few hundred voices. After a great volume of praise rolled heavenward, there came an atmosphere vibrant with the sense of the Divine as prayer was offered. I never heard Gipsy Smith before, and I was not prejudiced in his favour. But his simplicity, his directness, his power of speaking straight home to the heart, made me captive. Here was a master of crowd-psychology. The Jesus whom this man preached was the elder brother, the lover of men, the saviour from self. When the preacher asked those who desired to follow and obey Jesus to stand up, they rose in hundreds. It almost seemed as if the whole congregation were on their feet. The difficulty when every force seemed to lift one up was in continuing to sit still. This is the only mission that can to-day be effective—the mission in which the mysterious powers latent subconsciously in man are directed heavenward. Instead of weak, isolated, competitive missions, if the churches would organise home-missions after this order.... There in Pittsburg, as in every city where men such as Gipsy Smith exercise their ministry, the first requisite is that the churches organise to provide the herd. Without the herd, the herd-instinct cannot operate. First provide the crowd, and then the masters of crowd-psychology can turn their faces heavenward. It will be a poor ruined world if the crowd be left much longer as the monopoly of the devil. The laws of crowd-psychology, which can crucify a Christ and turn an ancient civilisation into carnage and animalism, can also shape humanity to the noblest ends. By these same laws self-sacrifice, love, heroism, idealism can make their irresistible appeal. Along this line victory will come.

CHAPTER VII

LET US HAVE PEACE

It was to attend a Congress of Churches that I crossed the Atlantic, but it is not listening to speeches that gives a realisation of any country. It is when wandering about the streets, sitting in cafés, listening in a smoking-car, or talking to a man in a hotel lounge that one forms some impression of the atmosphere which Americans breathe. It has been asserted, doubtless with truth, that human aberrations are a misplaced worship. That happiness which men were created to find in fellowship with the Highest, they seek in base and sensual forms. Drunkenness, on this theory, is a species of misdirected worship. If this be granted, then, Americans are of all nations the most devout. They worship the vast in every form. At Pittsburg you could hear a man rolling out statistics of millions of tons of steel a year; of harbour dues, though the city is far from the sea, that put even London and Glasgow in the shade; and as he speaks you feel that he has a thrill approaching adoration. He is on his knees before the greatest he knows. It is the same in everything. A town of 14,000 inhabitants in 1840 is now a city of a million. He rolls the figures as if they were a mystic ritual. Everything with which he has to do must be the greatest on the earth.

I

It was, however, in New York that one came to the inner shrine of American idealism. I had stayed for two days in the academic calm of Princeton, had heard Lord Bryce lecture in iced and polished and classic phrases on the age-long problem of Church and State; had spoken to two hundred theological students who might just be in Oxford or Edinburgh, for their eyes were just the same—the eyes of youth, who perennially believe that they at least were born to put this old world right. (That is the wonderful feeling that keeps pulpits filled—the feeling that however much the message has been spurned and others have failed, yet I cannot fail—glorious dream of youth!) From that atmosphere of reposeful idealism I was suddenly projected into the midst of New York. It was a bewildering experience. A friend who knew his way in the maze guided me to the Pennsylvania hotel, 'The biggest hotel in the world, with 2200 baths!' I found a room on the twentieth storey, served by an 'express' service of lifts. I could enter into the feelings of the countryman who, descending in one of those for the first time and seeing floor after floor flash past, murmured, 'Thank God, I am safe so far.' Having secured our 'baths' we went forth to see New York by night.

Straight as an arrow my friend brought me to the spots where the full blaze of the illumined streets burst into view. On every hand the street fronts blazed with multi-coloured lights. Rainbows of dazzling splendour spanned the avenues. Above every sky-scraper, darkening the stars, letters of fire proclaimed 'The Greatest Boot Emporium in the World' or 'The Vastest Store in all the Universe.' St. John in his dreams of apocalyptic splendour in Patmos could never have dreamed anything weirder than this. Far as the eye could see down Fifth Avenue the quivering lights proclaimed to the silent stars: 'We are the people—the greatest on the earth!' But, after all, the world is but a tenth-rate little gutta-percha ball in the immensity of infinitude, and it was a comfort to think that the constellations were not impressed. On our way back we rested in a 'Soda-Fountain' refreshment room where we sucked nectar through straws. 'This,' said my friend, 'was a notorious saloon before the war, and here are we, two douce parsons, drinking in all the phylacteries of respectability.' That, on the whole, was the most wonderful thing we saw that night in New York. But as I looked from the dizzy height of my room in the sky-scraper, out on that city of glittering light, I seemed to realise what it meant. That building of monstrous height, these proclamations that darkened the heavens, making the stars but a background for vaunting—what are they but the pursuit of the ideal; the scaling of heaven by force; the soul laying hold on immensity by both hands. It is humanity on its knees before the wrong altar.

II

It is the same when the Great War is recalled, as it inevitably is every hour. To the American his share looms so vast that he is convinced he won the war. Among certain classes 'We won the war' has become a watchword. 'My brother last year travelled through Italy and France and part of Germany,' a typical American will confide in you, 'and he met a German officer, and this German told him that they thought little of the English and less of the French, but that when the Americans came in they recognised their masters and quitted at once.' Hereupon a quiet man in a corner begins to talk. 'We air a wonderful nation, sir, and that's a sure thing,' he nasalises; 'we had only 50,000 casualties, and you had a million, and the French a million and a half, and the Russians perhaps two millions, and the Italians half a million—say five millions in all among the Europeans. My friend says we won the war with 50,000 casualties! His idea seems to be that an American is worth a hundred of his brethren in Europe. It is the atmosphere here, sir. We air a great nation, sir.' Upon this the first eyes the second speaker askance. But a Canadian takes up the tale. 'There was an Englishman down in Florida this summer and he went bathing,' thus the Canadian. 'There was a poster forbidding bathing at a particular beach; but there the Englishman, having donned his bathing suit, plunged in. The watcher of the beach rushed to him on his return to shore and reprimanded him for disobeying orders. "Oh! I am all right, for I took precautions," was the answer. "What precautions?" exclaimed the watcher, at once professionally interested. And the bather turned round and showed his newly-bought bathing suit. On one side it bore the stars and stripes and on the other the legend "We won the war." Pointing to these he said, "I was perfectly safe, for no shark that ever swam in the ocean would swallow that!"' ... The Canadian can beat the Yankee at his own game. He just pricks the tube and you hear the wind whizzing. But in a few years nobody in the States outside the ranks of the learned will know anything about any one's sufferings and heroisms in the Great War except their own. Just as to-day it is a surprise to a German to learn that Wellington won Waterloo, so in the future it will be a surprise to an American to learn that Britain and France by rivers of their blood won the Great War. 'We won the war' has only begun as yet to run its course.

III

It was, however, at Mount Vernon, sixteen miles south of Washington, that I seemed to be nearest to the soul of America. It was with a quiet thankfulness that I left the city behind and went on pilgrimage to Mount Vernon, the home of George Washington. There the scenes amid which the Father of his country moved and had his being are unchanged. In the city, the Washington monument, a shaft of white marble rising to a height of '555 feet 5 1/8 inches,' confronts one's eyes at the end of every vista. But here no monument challenges the world by its height. The plain, wooden building, painted to resemble stone, with a piazza extending along the whole front, consisting of two storeys and an attic with dormer windows, surmounted by a small cupola and an ancient weathervane, is just as it was when Washington lived and died. In these rooms with the tables and chairs and bed and pictures, and the books (duplicates mostly), just as they were a hundred and fifty years ago, there were dreamed dreams that have changed half the world. Out of this farm-house came the impulse and the power wherewith 'The embattled farmers stood and fired the shot heard around the world.'

There could be found few spots on earth in which one could better muse on the mutability of earthly affairs than in these rooms tenanted by ghosts. Here in the main hall is the key of the Bastille, sent by Lafayette from Paris as a gift to Washington after the capture of the prison in 1789. 'Give me leave, my dear General,' wrote Lafayette, 'to present you with a picture of the Bastille, just as it looked a few days after I ordered its demolition, with the main key of the fortress of despotism. It is a gift which I owe as a son to my adopted country, as an aide-de-camp to my General, as a missionary of liberty to its patriarch.' No nation ever owed so great a debt for its liberty as the United States owed to France. George Washington won the War of Independence because half the people of Britain sympathised with him, knowing that he was fighting their battle for liberty as well as his own; but mainly because France espoused his cause on sea and land, and sent him money, and men, and leaders such as Lafayette. But in the realm of international politics gratitude has no place. When France in 1914 faced the menace of overwhelming and final destruction; when Belgium, to whose independence the United States was a signatory at the Hague Convention, was overrun, the Government at Washington did not even enter a protest, and the President still addressed the Kaiser as 'great and good friend.' While France that won her liberty for America was for three years in Gethsemane, the States were 'too proud to fight.' As late as 1917 there was the famous speech about 'peace without victory.' It was only when a Presidential Election was gained by 'the Man who kept us out of the war,' and when the interests of the States on the high seas were threatened with ruin, that the Americans at last entered the fray. If Britain had acted as the States did, France to-day would have been the conscript appendage of Germany. When the American Ambassador in London declared in a candid moment that America came into the war for 'her own interests,' the resolutions passed and the speeches made disowning him were amazing. That key of the Bastille there in Mount Vernon is a monument of international ingratitude. There is no reason to narcotise ourselves into believing that poor humanity has been changed for ever in this year of grace at Washington.

IV

To-day Mount Vernon is a shrine, and a sky-scraping monument dominates Washington, but George Washington learned in his own day the lesson that in politics there is no gratitude. The founder of the great Republic did not escape the common fate. He was accused as President of drawing more than his salary, of aping at monarchy; there were hints of the guillotine being needed; until at last the scurrilous attacks drove Washington to declare at a Cabinet meeting in 1793 that he would rather be in his grave than in his present position. It is said that at the end he would have preferred to seek reunion with Britain. (An American lecturer was howled down in New York two years ago for venturing to refer to that!) This at least is sure, that Washington was glad to end his days in the peace of Mount Vernon. If this may seem incredible one has only to think of the fate of Clemenceau, of Venizelos, or of Woodrow Wilson. There is to-day in Washington a living monument of national ingratitude. Whatever may be thought of many of the acts of President Wilson, of his leaving France to her fate until he won his election to the second term of office by the help of the anti-British and pacifist votes, yet posterity will undoubtedly acclaim him as Lincoln now is acclaimed. It was he who not only, with the dreamers of all the years, dreamed the dream of perpetual peace, but by his unbending will-power forced the nations of Europe to place that dream, materialised in the League of Nations, in the forefront of the Treaty of Versailles. That was one of those epoch-making events on which the history of the world turns. It is idle to think that the coming generations will not place the man who did that among the greatest of the human race. And yet to-day his own countrymen can find no words strong enough to express their contempt and dislike. There is no more pathetic figure in all the world. A shattered body gains him no respite from abuse. When the broken man drove for the last time from the White House to his own home—the burden at last laid down—a demonstration organised by the League of Nations Union cheered him at his gate. They would not go away until he spoke. He was taken to a window, and after saying a few words he pointed to his throat, in token that he could not further reply to the ovation. History can scarcely parallel that tragedy. But Woodrow Wilson can comfort himself with the thought that the hosannas will rise in chorus when he is dead. George Washington has now a monument 555 feet high; a hundred years hence Woodrow Wilson will have a monument 666 feet high. The generations of those who garnish tombs never fail. 'I tremble for my country,' said President Jefferson, 'when I remember that God is just.'

V

The world has raised a chorus of rejoicing over the results of the Conference at Washington. While we rejoice at the prospect of reducing the number of battleships, we can only rejoice with trembling. (It is America, who had the Japanese navy on the brain, that has the greatest cause to rejoice.) But agreements and treaties are not going to save us. The crucial question is not the form and context of a treaty, but rather whether there is among men sufficient truth and righteousness to fulfil its terms. The warfare of the future will be a warfare of chemistry. (According to a statement ascribed to Edison, the whole population of London can in the future be wiped out in eight hours by poison gas!) Is there a possibility of restricting laboratories and the massing of deadly germs? The men who will release the energy in an atom will be able to destroy a world. If we look at facts we shall not be drugged by oratory. 'Rhetoric,' said Theodore Roosevelt, 'is a poor substitute for the habit of looking facts resolutely in the face.' The facts confronting us are ominous enough. Twice recently one of the greatest of nations has thrown over the signature of its Supreme Head and its Secretary of State. The United States repudiated its President and refused to ratify the League of Nations; and not only that, but refused also to ratify the Agreement made with France and Britain to secure France against future aggression. The present misery and unrest in Europe are largely due to the failure of one hundred and ten millions of the English-speaking race to honour the signature of their Chief. The best of them bewail it, and say that it is the fault of their political system. Under the worst system of European government such events would be impossible.

But though the failure to ratify treaties be grievous, yet the failure to observe treaties duly ratified is still more grievous. And the history of our relations with the States is largely the history of broken treaties. There was the famous Clayton-Bulwer Treaty of 1850 regarding the Panama Canal; it was repudiated in 1880, and its history since is a history of broken agreements. There have been so many conferences, so many agreements, so many treaties since the days of the Holy Alliance to the days of The Hague, and the end has always been the same. In 1916 Mr. Elihu Root made a speech in the American Senate, the echoes of which will ring round the world in the coming years. The burden of his sorrow was shame for his country's repudiation of their obligation to protect Belgium. Here are some sentences:—

'Wherever there was respect for law, it revolted against the wrong done to Belgium. Wherever there was true passion for liberty, it blazed out for Belgium. Wherever there was humanity it mourned for Belgium.... The law protecting Belgium was our law and the law of every civilised country.... We had played our part, in conjunction with other civilised nations, in making that law.... Moreover, that law was written into a solemn and formal Convention, signed and ratified by Germany, and Belgium and France, and the United States.... When Belgium was invaded, that Agreement was binding, not only morally, but strictly and technically, because there was then no nation a party to the war which was not also a party to the Convention. The invasion of Belgium was a breach of contract with us for the maintenance of a law of nations.... The American Government failed to rise to the demands of a great occasion. Gone were the old love of justice, the old passion for liberty, the old sympathy with the oppressed, the old ideals of an America helping the world towards a better future, and there remained in the eyes of mankind only solicitude for trade and profit and prosperity and wealth.'

Yes, humanity might mourn for Belgium, and the States stand aloof in spite of its plighted word, but what of that when an election had to be won and the Irish vote conciliated! The world being what it is there can be no hope of deliverance along the road of treaties. There can be no salvation by parchments. You cannot make a treaty when there is no sense of truth and honour. You cannot make a treaty with paganism. There is no truth or honour there for a treaty to rest on. And the world is still overwhelmingly pagan. Europe may have been baptized and America also, but Asia still dreams that its day will return. Japan is haunted by the dreams of Potsdam, and the hunger of empire is in her eyes. China, India, Africa, and the Turk are not yet even baptized! And yet people think that we have arrived at last within sight of the millennium. The characteristic of humanity is its credulous simplicity. Men cannot rid themselves of the fond belief that they can reform the jungle by manicuring the tiger's claws.

VI

The march of events is the proof that the woe of humanity is too deeply seated to be healed by any human salve. There is no balm in any Gilead for these wounds. The first step towards the rehabilitation of the world would be the mutual cancelling of the nations' debts to each other. The United States alone makes this impossible. Money that we borrowed for our allies, and which we cannot recover from our allies, America insists that we pay. And yet that money was spent to save America as well as ourselves. To realise that one has only to think what would have happened if Germany had won? The greatest day in the history of Scotland was when the German fleet, its crimes against the laws of Neptune for ever ended, came sailing into the Forth to surrender. Through the mist that shrouded it there never moved a procession so humiliating and so woeful. Judgment at last overtook the murderers who gloated over the *Lusitania*! But supposing Germany had won, what then? The first condition would have been the surrender of the British fleet at Kiel. And we would have no choice; for a starving nation must sacrifice everything to feed its children. But what would have happened then? Think of the Emperor William master of the British and French fleets as well as his own. What would have become of the Monroe Doctrine next morning? What would have become of the scores he had to settle about the supplying of munitions to his foes? In face of the might confronting her, America would have been helpless. New York would have been given to the flames if America came not to heel. We saved the great Republic as well as France and ourselves. And now, having given our sons and our treasure, we are being bled white that we may pay America for the munitions which we used in her defence. These payments are earmarked for the payment of American war-pensions! The world has never seen so grotesque a situation. The protected and the delivered demand that their protectors and deliverers should pay for the privilege of protecting and delivering them! What is at the back of so preposterous a state of things? It is this, that there is the shadow of a Presidential Election looming ahead, and the cancelling of the debts guaranteed by Britain would be unpopular. One can quite realise the use the Irish orators would make of that. We forget that Anglophobia is still the staple of American history as taught in her schools. The Boston Tea Party and the War of Independence were due to British vices and the triumph of

American virtues. To cancel the debts for which such a nation is responsible would be to repudiate the makers of America! ... What is required, of course, is the right education of the American democracy. Schools should teach that it is impossible in so imperfect a world that all the right can be on one side. Yet that is how history is taught, not only there but here. Our foes also were always wrong! There will be no peace in the world until the spirit of spread-eagleism is replaced by that of meekness; until nations and men realise that we are members one of another, and that we are here to help and serve each other. Until that new spirit breathes through the masses of humanity, there will be war. And we shall have to endure. We who saved America must pay for the privilege of saving her; and we must do it while every opportunity of doing so is snatched from us. A tariff that will exclude our goods has been established; the only way left to pay is by acting as carriers on the seas! Now we are to be driven from that service by nationally subsidised mercantile American fleets! And yet we must pay! ... If anything could waken humanity to the fact that the conversion of the people can alone save the world, it would be this. Missionaries to convert the hearts of the American voters is the world's supreme need.

VII

One of the most impressive sights in New York is the tomb of General Grant. Its site overlooking the deep-gorged Hudson river is most impressive. It is a square building of white granite without and white marble within, surmounted by a cupola with Ionic columns. Above the door, between two figures emblematic of peace and war, are inscribed the words, 'Let us have peace.' These are the closing words of his letter accepting the Presidency. Grant had a right to use the words, for he was a great peace-maker. He made peace by conquering the forces of disruption. He kept stubbornly at it. But when he won at last he would not humiliate Lee by taking his sword from him; and when he was told that Lee's men owned their own horses—'Let them keep them,' said Grant; 'they will need them for the spring ploughing.' Nor would he allow any salvos of victory. 'We are all citizens of the same Republic,' said he; 'let us have peace.' To-day the whole world is one Republic woven together by the mighty shuttles of steamships, airships, and wireless. In that world there can be no hermit nation. In that world, 'let us have peace.' In the Governor's garden at the base of the slope that leads to the citadel, in Quebec, there is an obelisk that stirs the heart. It is a monument to Wolfe and Montcalm. The one died content that he had won a dominion greater than he knew for the nation that he loved; the other, dying, comforted himself with the thought that he did not live to see the surrender of Quebec. There, these two heroic souls, near the scene of their heroism, share a common monument. The inscription is the most beautiful I know:—

Mortem, Virtus, Communem,
Famam Historia
Monumentum Posteritas
Dedit.

'Valour gave them a common death; history a common fame; posterity a common monument.' That obelisk visualises the hope of the future. It would indeed be a miserable world in which men went on hating for ever. Only the spirit of Him who for the love of men stooped to a cross can dig the grave of hate and war at last. When the world shall awake from its nightmare and shall listen to Him, then the world will have peace.

VIII

When I shall have forgotten all else, I shall remember a morning spent in Trinity Church, New York. The oldest grave in the graveyard surrounding it is that of a little child, Richard Churcher, 'who died the 5 of April 1681 of age 5 years and 5 months.' The child's name has outlived the city; for the old city is gone. A few years ago the spire of Trinity Church was a landmark. Now they are completely hidden by the buildings of enormous height that surround them. By contrast the church and spire look like toys. One building soars to 724 feet—49 storeys, with elevators rising 41 storeys in one minute, and express elevators 30 storeys in 30 seconds! Even St. Paul's Cathedral surrounded by buildings such as the Woolworth, rising to 800 feet, would be dwarfed into significance, and Trinity Church is small compared to St. Paul's. It is when one ponders such a scene that one realises what it is that is wrong with the world. The towers and pinnacles of Mammon soar everywhere high above the puny sanctuaries of faith. The evangel of the Carpenter of Nazareth is jostled aside and crowded out. What the world has to do is to make room once more for love and self-sacrifice—for idealism. That is the only road to salvation. Nobody knows that better than the American. He likes to listen to oratory about world-peace; but when the oratory is done he smiles. 'We might as well,' says he, 'try to lift ourselves by our bootlaces.' And that is the moral of it all.

* * * * *

The United States refused the mandate for Armenia, and the mandate for Constantinople, and dishonoured the signature of its chief magistrate guaranteeing the security of France. To-day the blood of the slain cries to Heaven, and Britain is left alone holding the gates of Europe against a race whose only rule is government by massacre. And from America the Press reports a cablegram to the Prime Minister:—'Win civilisation's everlasting appreciation by keeping the brutes out of Europe. Americans expect every

Englishman to do his duty.' What a strange species of humour! In very truth the regeneration of the world's democracies is the only road to peace.

CHAPTER VIII

THE WAY OF PEACE

The supreme need of the world to-day is peace. Europe is sinking into the morass of despair because across their frontiers a dozen nations drilled and armed are watching each other with sullen eyes. From the shores of the Pacific to the long wash of Australasian seas everywhere it is the same. Civilisation is perishing; but it is a civilisation armed to the teeth that is awaiting its obsequies. Every newspaper proclaims the one need is Peace. The Conference on disarmament has but one word to express the sum of all its desires—Peace. There must be some stupendous barrier in the way when all this yearning and endless talking fail to reach the goal of humanity's striving. However eagerly the nations pursue it, peace seems to be for ever a receding horizon. If on one spot of an anguished world statesmen confer as to the things that make for peace, yet behind their fortified frontiers the nations are still sharpening their swords. It is, as it has ever been, a mad world.

I

There must be some hidden cause of this failure of humanity to work out its own deliverance. And our duty is to find out that cause. It is quite possible to make an idol even of peace. Peace is not necessarily the supreme good. If there have been wars which call for repentance and humiliation on the part of those who waged them, there have been again and again periods of peace which call for even deeper humiliation and keener repentance. If we have waged war when we ought to have been at peace, we have as often been at peace when we ought to have waged war. Time and again, a generation ago, we heard of Armenians being massacred. But we kept the peace. There never was a more disgraceful peace in the history of the world, and awful has been the price that we have paid for it. To keep the peace when the innocent are being massacred is damnation. Peace is not then the supreme word in man's vocabulary. By mouthing it man often falls into the mire. There is a greater word by far, and that is—righteousness. The only peace worth having is the fruit of righteousness. That is why peace flies faster than its pursuers. The votaries of peace have forgotten that fruit does not grow without roots and soil. Eloquence can do much, but it cannot grow grapes without vines deep rooted in the soil. And peace is a fruit of the spirit deep rooted in righteousness. And the nations pursuing peace have forgotten that pilgrimages to Washington or The Hague may be good, but the supreme need of humanity is to go on pilgrimage to the fountains that will cleanse the heart. The deliverance of the world is not by way of renewed or remodelled treaties, but by the old, old way of renewed and converted souls.

II

How has peace ever come to men? It has come in one way only—the way of the renewed spirit. I have been reading again the wonderful story of this Scotland of ours, and that old, simple truth has come home to me afresh. The problem that confronted Scotland in the dawn of its history was how to unify and pacify warring tribes that were ceaselessly drenching the land with blood. And the way the problem was solved here is the way in which alone it can be solved on the greater stage of the whole world. Fourteen hundred years ago there was no Scotland anywhere on the map. There were four kingdoms in North Britain—the Picts north of the Grampians, the Britons in Strathclyde, the Angles in the Lothians and southward to the Tweed, and in Kintyre a small and feeble colony of Scots who had crossed from Ireland. (In those days a Scot was invariably an Irishman.) In those distressful days wars in North Britain were as common as strikes are now, and women went forth to battle along with the men. And they were wars of extermination—without mercy. Out of that welter how did unity and peace come? The uniter and pacifier came out of Ireland. The Scots in Kintyre were Christians, and the pagan Picts under King Brude inflicted on them a shattering defeat. It looked as if Christianity were on the eve of being stamped out in Kintyre. To Columba in Ireland there came the cry of his kinsmen's woe—'Come over and help us.' To a man burning with ardour and longing for new fields to conquer for his Master, that cry was like a bugle summoning to battle. He came to their help, but not with spears and arrows. He came with the might of the Cross. The greatness of the man is revealed in the fact that instead of material weapons he went straight to the fountain-head of the misery. He realised that there was only one way of salvation for the Christian Scots in Kintyre, and that was by converting to Christ the wild people in the North that had braved the Roman arms and were still in their primitive savagery. In those days to convert a clan one had first to convert the chief; to convert a nation one had first to convert the king. The goal towards which St. Columba set his face was the castle of King Brude at Inverness. Iona was but the base for the great campaign that was to make North Britain safe for Christians. If to-day the problem be how to make the world safe for democracy (though the problem is really greater—how to produce a democracy worth the sacrifice of making the world safe for it), in the sixth century the problem was how to make Scotland safe for Christ.

III

The greatest story in our history is that which tells how Columba made his venture of faith and conquered. He never lacked courage this man. 'Do you think, Columba, shall I be saved?' asked the King of Ireland. 'Certainly not,' answered Columba, 'unless you break off from your sins, repent, and be converted.' The courage wherewith he faced his kinsfolk, with that same courage he now faced his enemy. We can see his galley sailing up Loch Linnhe with the Cross at the masthead, and the face of the leader set like a flint. He would go to the stronghold of paganism. Up the great glen the little band trudged with death lurking behind every bush, but there was never a thought of faltering. In vain did King Brude bar his gates against him. No walls can shut out the Spirit, no gates of iron can debar the Word living and powerful. Outside the gates Columba and his band begin to chant a Psalm— 'We have heard with our ears, O God, our fathers have told us, what work Thou didst in their days ... how Thou didst drive out the heathen with Thy hand....' And as that voice of his rolled like thunder the King and the people 'were affrighted with fear intolerable.' The gates were flung open and King Brude surrendered to the ambassador of Christ. The wild race, whom the legions of Rome could not subdue, were conquered by an unarmed man. What a light must have been in that man's eye: what a fire in his heart! From that day Scotland was safe for the followers of Christ, and the little band of Christians in Kintyre could now sleep peacefully at night, for King Brude was learning the law of love and the way of peace. From that day the good seed was sown broadcast over all the land. That dauntless messenger traversed sombre, uncharted gulfs, trod his way along rock-strewn sounds, and the darkness of the centuries faded before the Cross that gleamed at the masthead. The Picts became Christians, and in due course united with the Christian Scots in Kintyre, and Scotland found a name. In time the Angles and Strathclyde were merged in the unity of the Kingdom of Scotland. There came first the unity of one ideal, of one law, of one faith—and out of that there came the four kingdoms merged at last in the unity of the one Kingdom of Scotland. Until at last, after weary centuries, the sounds of war hushed into silence: clan no longer lifted up sword against clan; brethren in Christ could no longer slay one another. Peace lay at last like a golden shaft across all the land. One fearless unarmed man faced a king with the weapons of the Spirit, sowed the harvest which we are now reaping.

IV

It is only by that road that humanity can come at last to the great goal of universal peace. It is the road that nations are unwilling to tread. They still are following the mirage that has strewn the deserts of time with the bleached skeletons of those who set out to reach it. The mirage is salvation by treaties. That idol has had hecatombs offered on its altars, and unless there comes a change it will have hecatombs in the future. If there be no truth and righteousness in the heart that signs, then treaties are valueless. The history of the centuries is the proof of their futility. The treaties of to-day can no more save than the treaties of all the yesterdays. For the nations that sign cannot trust each other. In the hearts of the nations there is not throned that righteousness which can be trusted.

The world's sickness is of the soul. What the nations need is that truth and righteousness be enthroned in their midst. Without that, peace is only the scum on the surface of the foul and stagnant pool. And the witness of the centuries is that righteousness is the fruit of the vision of God. The foundation of righteousness is the realisation of the ceaseless operation of the laws whose source is God. If only the vision of God could blaze forth before the eyes of democracies as it blazed forth before the eyes of King Brude, then the way of peace would open up for groaning humanity. How can there be lasting peace in a world of conflicting ideals? Can Christianity be at peace with Mohammedanism stained with the blood of millions of Armenians; with paganism still brooding over the ideal of an empire based on force? Can the ideals of unselfish service and of pride and greed lie down in peace together? There can be no peace until humanity is brought into a unity of the soul—of allegiance to one King, of obedience to one law. The only hand worthy to wield the sceptre of the world is the hand that was nailed to a Cross. What the world has to realise is that the Manger overthrows the Cæsars, and that the road leading to a Cross is the way of peace. When we shall send forth over all the world men endued with the spirit of St. Columba, then there will be hope of the world. But that is the last thing we think of. We fondly believe that while we ourselves are sinking back into the mire we shall be able to lift the world up into light; while we ourselves turn our backs on the Prince of Peace, that we will bestow peace on the world. It is the weirdest of all obsessions. When William Ewart Gladstone was once asked how a man of his intellect could listen to such dull sermons, he answered— 'I go to church because I love England.' There is a wider motive—'I go to church because I love the world, because I can hear there a law that men should love one another with a love that stoops to a Cross, by which alone the world can be saved.' It is vain for nations that forsake the worship of a God of love to spend their days devising schemes for bringing peace to a ruined world. For there is no way of peace save one—the way of love. No nation has as yet tried that way. And there is no sign that they mean to try it. The world waits for the man who will convince it that the new order must be based on fraternity and not on fighting. But the world will applaud him instantly. Fraternity—that's the word! Most excellent! But when the new Columba will go on to show that fraternity without a Fatherhood to rest on is meaningless and powerless; that humanity can only realise its brotherhood in a common Father—even God. Then the world will once more shrug its shoulders. 'This is the same old wheeze,' it will say—and go its way. For we have no longer any use for God. That is the root of our misery.

CHAPTER IX

NO ROOM

There is an old Gaelic proverb that says: 'Where there is heart-room there also is house-room.' There was room enough in that mean inn for the farmers with their pouches filled with money for the tax, for the soldiers that swaggered with the pride of empire, for the village-talebearers with their rude jests; but for a poor woman in the hour of her need there was no room. She was shut out because there was not found in that inn any with heart big enough to make room for her. What was she anyway?—a mere chattel; and what her child?—already there were too many children; and the only course to adopt was to let most of them die! And so at its dawn we can see what a mighty change Christianity has made in the world. Though the mother and the Child were shut out of the inn and consigned to the asses' stall, yet because of that mother and Child womanhood is to-day honoured and childhood most precious. To-day, in whatever land on which the shadow of the Cross has fallen, there is heart-room and house-room for mother and child.

I

As one reads the old beautiful story, this foot-note that explains how the Founder of Christianity was born in a stable because 'there was no room for them in the inn' stirs the mind with a wistful poignancy. The book slips down on the knees and the imagination awakes. The essence of nineteen centuries of Christian history is here. The web of all the centuries is woven after the one pattern. Shut out at His birth, His fate has been the same ever since. He came with the message of humanity's renewal. He proclaimed the most revolutionary doctrine ever preached to men—that the pariahs of humanity, publicans, sinners, slaves, those ignorant of the law and therefore accursed, were all the sons of God; and that only one law was requisite, that men should love one another with a love that gleamed red with sacrificial blood. But what have men done with this evangel? They have shut it out! It was too beautiful for their gross hearts and their self-clouded eyes. It was also very difficult. It required the changed heart and the transfigured life. And that has always been most difficult—to transmute the self-centred into the God-centred and all it means. So men set themselves to circumvent that demand for the surrendered heart—and they offered the surrendered brain. That is quite easy. They formulated logical propositions setting forth that thus and thus God acted, and they said—'Believe this and be saved, or disbelieve and be damned!' Christianity that came into the world as spirit and life became mere intellectual gymnastics! And with the name of the Lord of Love on their lips

Christians cheerfully burnt each other because their definitions differed.... What an amazing fate to overtake the most beautiful thing that ever was seen on the earth! ... A Borgia sits on the throne of St. Peter; Calvin burns Servetus; the Jesuit exterminates his opponents; the Covenanter proclaims that he prefers to die than to live and see 'this intolerable toleration'; and all the time the Lord Jesus Christ is shut out. Not wholly shut out, however, for He has in every age found a shelter and a welcome in the stables and the sheds, among the ragged, the mean, and the outcasts of humanity.

II

It is not only in the great organisations that bear His name that there has often been found no room for the Christ; but still less has there been found room for Him in the social order. This great revolutionary identifies Himself so closely with humanity, that He declares that whosoever receives a little child and loves it receives and loves Him. How then do we deal with the Founder of Christianity as He comes to us in the form of a little child, saying, 'Receive Me'? ... This is the way we deal with Him. Every five minutes of the day a baby dies somewhere in the United Kingdom. There are districts in great cities where two hundred out of one thousand perish in the first year of life. A third of the possible population die in the years of childhood. The horrors of war are small compared to the horrors of peace, to which we have become so inured that we scarce notice them. We have taken the sunshine and the fresh air and the starlight from millions of our fellow citizens and shut them up in barracks and surrounded them with forces of degeneration, and have provided them a narcotic for their misery, so that womanhood becomes degraded and childhood pines and dies. Still, after nineteen centuries, Jesus Christ is shut out from the social order we have laboriously created. And we celebrate Christmas Day without so much as a sense of incongruity between our beliefs and our actions.

II

One of the weirdest symptoms of decay in our day is the way the whole social system seems to have conspired to shut out the child. In the last years property-owners had one condition that was unaltered: they would not let their houses to tenants with children. 'How many children and how old are they?' was the deciding question that always shut the door. The coming of a baby was often the signal that brought an ejectment warrant. The penalty for bringing a child into the world was being thrown into the street. The men who filled the inn at Bethlehem with mirth nineteen centuries ago have had a mighty multitude who shared their spirit. Rents have been to them more to be desired than babies.

Here is an advertisement that appeared in the *Daily Chronicle* of 29th May 1917: 'Chapel-keepers, man and wife (no children), for large Congregational church, Central London; must be total abstainers ... 5 rooms, coal and light provided.—Write ———, hon. secretary, ... E.C. 4.' I forbear giving the name of the Christian church that provides five rooms for its 'keeper' and slams the door in the face of the child. (The curious can find it in the files.) Even in this day, when the child is so precious to the race, one can see unblushing advertisements for gardeners and lodge-keepers with the clause 'no children.' That the children of this world should act so is deplorable; but that the children of the light should have 'five rooms,' and in them all no place for a cradle—that suggests doom. Think of that congregation hailing, with songs of rapture, the coming of the Child; the preacher getting dewy over the callousness of the inn in Bethlehem—and their own servants forbidden a child! ... It was something like that which caused a prophet of old to exclaim—'Judgment begins in the House of God.'

IV

At this Christmastide what we need most is to make room for the Child. People are ever ready to make room for that which they recognise to be precious. The most precious thing on earth is goodness. Give any mother her choice of her son being rich and a rogue, or poor and good; she will choose poverty. There is no power that builds up men and women in unselfishness and goodness but the power that is radiated from Him whose life on earth began in a manger. We must, if need be, cast away our costliest treasures that we may make room.... In very truth He cannot now be shut out altogether. No contumely will drive Him hence. It is different now from the day when a woman groped her way in agony to the asses and the stall. Different now, for He comes in through the closed doors. That is how the world has not been able to destroy Christianity; and that is how the Child conquers at the last.

CHAPTER X

DOMINION FROM SEA TO SEA

No part of the Empire rendered the cause of the world's soul in the world war greater service than Canada. When the clouds of chlorine gas were let loose it was the Canadians who stopped the gap through which the torrent of destruction was flowing. And the question the wounded men gasped out of tortured throats and lungs was not 'Shall I live?' but 'Did the Huns get through?' In the great host that at last swept the wolves back to their lair, the Canadians were foremost. 'We pledge ourselves solemnly before God to keep faith with our fallen comrades,' wrote General Currie to Sir Robert Borden, and nobly did they fulfil the pledge. To-day when a citizen of the States begins to demonstrate how his countrymen won the war, a Canadian produces the official statistics from his pocket and shows how the ten millions of Canada gave more of their sons over to death and wounds than the total casualties of the one hundred and ten millions in the States. And it is not surprising that Canada should have a clear vision of the ideal of duty. The very name that their country bears lifts that young nation into the fellowship of the highest ideal. When a name was discussed for the new confederation an inspiration came to Sir Leonard Tilley as he read the eighth verse of the seventy-second psalm: 'He shall have dominion also from sea to sea, and from the river unto the ends of the earth,' and on his initiative the name Dominion was adopted. Not for Canada alone but for the whole Empire that name sets forth the only ideal. The cry of 'World-dominion or death' can only be overcome at last by the watchword 'God-dominion and Life.'

I

It is difficult for men to learn the lesson of their own most bitter experience. Only when the Cross stands far back across the years does its meaning and purpose faintly gleam on the minds of men. It need be no matter for surprise that men who did not themselves stand in the breach of death should be unable to articulate the master-word of the future. That great word will be— Spirit. What the world gazed on for four years of woe was the triumph of the spirit. To the men who, footsore and limping, marched back from Mons, defeat was incredible—their souls knew not the word. And because victory, even as they retreated, was in their souls, they swept the enemy back from the gates of Paris. For four years in mud and misery and defeat the soul endured and triumphed. It was the greatest of all the soldiers of France who said to his body as it shrank in his first battle: 'Tremblest thou? If thou knewest the dangers into which I shall this day carry thee, thou wouldest tremble!' Often and often in these four years the poor worn suffering body said, 'I have had enough—enough of mud and vermin—I am fed up; I will do no more,' but when the call of duty came the soul said to the body, 'I will make you face it, make you go through with it'; and the soul compelled the body to charge into the very face of death. It was the spark of the Divine in the soul that enabled our brothers to conquer the shrinking of flesh and blood and so to conquer the foe. It is in the measure that armies are souls that armies conquer. And it has been the same at home in castle and cot-house. We have but to think of the wives and mothers.

'They let them go forth at the wheels
Of the guns and denied not. But then the surprise
When one sits quiet alone! Then one weeps, then one kneels,
God! how the house feels.'

However deeply the iron pierced, there was never a thought of defeat being even possible. And when the call came the women toiled in the factories, and the ammunition dumps were their spirit materialised. At home and in the battle-line the final destiny of every nation depends upon the soul.

II

Still more is the mastery of this word apparent when we consider the future destiny of the world. One result of the world's blood-bath is that all thoughtful men are asking, How can the world be saved in the future? And multitudes discuss the way of the world's salvation by a League of Nations or other method. By parchments and signatures the world is to be saved! All that is but the folly with which men have deceived themselves in all ages. The folly is apparent when we ask, Whence do wars spring? They spring from greed and lust and ambition—from the life surrendered to evil. We speak of the horror of war; what we should speak of is the horror of wickedness. For war is only a symptom, not the disease. What all these weary discussions about 'Leagues to make an end of war,' and the new watchword 'No more war,' aim at is the doing away with the symptom—leaving the disease to run its deadly course. To suppress symptoms without removal of the hidden cause is the way of death. What the nations must face is the disease and its healing!

It is with nations as with individuals! How can a man protect himself against a thief. He can do it in three ways. He may (1) use force; or (2) he may make an agreement with the thief—enter into a treaty with him; or (3) he may endeavour to reform the thief. The first method is militarism and, whether in the form of armies or policemen, is costly and uncertain. The second only protects so long as the thief finds it convenient or in his own interest to keep it. Neither a burglar nor a robber-state can be warded off by treaties. The third alone provides a certain protection; the only safety is that the thief experience a change of spirit—be, in short, converted. 'Admirable,' said Cardinal Fleury, when a scheme for 'perpetual peace' was submitted to him; 'admirable, save for one omission—I find no provision for sending missionaries to convert the hearts of princes.' The day of princes is over, and the day of democracy has come. The first requisite of perpetual peace is that the nations of the world experience a change of heart and spirit—should repent. But in all the schemes for ending war there is no suggestion of sending missionaries to convert the world's democracies. France has 'extinguished the lights of heaven which none shall rekindle'; England, if the number of worshippers in the churches be any gauge, is rapidly sinking back into paganism; and across the Atlantic the United States is resolved to live unto itself alone, separating itself from the perishing nations; while on the Continent of Europe there is but one ritual: 'We did no wrong: we did not begin the war.' Missionaries to convert the democracies of the world—they are needed in legions. But such a need is not in all the thoughts of the orators. They can only think of forming leagues to abolish the vultures that swoop down on the carcases. They cannot realise that the only way to make an end of the swooping vulture is to make an end of carcases. Unless the world experiences a spiritual and moral renewal, any league that would secure it peace in the midst of its depravity would only secure its moral doom. It is manifest then that the only way to abolish war is to bring the body into subjection to the spirit. The way of salvation is the way of spiritual renewal. Love does not kill or poison, and humanity's feet need to be guided into the way of love. Along that road there is but the one guide: He who said 'I am the way.... Love as I have loved you.' The measure of that love is the Cross. And that is why the way to salvation leads through Calvary.... Peace will only come when the kingdoms of this world shall submit to that kingdom of the soul whose dominion is from sea to sea. 'I find a hundred little indications to reassure one that God comes,' writes H. G. Wells. 'The time draws near when mankind will awake ... and there shall be ... no leader but the one God of mankind.' But though Mr. Wells writes sentences so vital as that, yet when one asks him what God is—he is silent. Is He holy and righteous? Though Mr. Wells' God is but an abstraction, yet the truth remains. The coming of the Kingdom of God is the one hope of mankind—that Kingdom which Jesus preached. And the entrance into that Kingdom is by way of repentance and love and faith. When the soul of the world awakes to that, the day of deliverance shall have dawned.

III

This, then, must be the goal of human effort, to bring the nations of the world into such a unity of spirit that war will no longer be thinkable. But we, as a nation, can only do this if we ourselves bring our lives into conformity with the laws of righteousness. It is manifest that no amount of oratory will enable us to raise the world to any higher level than we have attained ourselves.

The first duty, then, is to see that we base our own lives on righteousness. The problem is how to bring to bear on the human heart those motives that will move it irresistibly towards righteousness. That road is not easy to travel and the choice of it means effort and travail. It means a battle against selfishness and self-seeking—a battle long-drawn-out. Why should men choose that conflict rather than ease and self-indulgence? There can be no reason save this: that God wills and enjoins righteousness. But does He? We know very little about God, and the strange thing is that the more knowledge that comes to us regarding Him, the more mysterious He becomes. But there is one thing that we do know with absolute certainty regarding God, and it is this—that all down the thousands of years of recorded history the power of the Unseen Ruler of the universe can be traced fighting against iniquity, burying corrupt nations under the avalanche, digging the grave for tyranny and corruption. The history of the world is the history of God making an end of crime. The way to destruction has been the way of iniquity. That God should have so ordered the universe that the stars in their courses fight against the Siseras, that all its forces are at last arrayed for the destruction of evil, is the proof that God is righteous and holy and that the passion in His heart is that His children should be righteous and holy. The world, as God means it, is the school for the training of men and women in goodness—and so in the image of God.... It is only the call of the Unseen Ruler as He summons His children to bring their lives into unison with Himself, that can turn the feet into the way of righteousness. There is no impelling force equal to the choice of good rather than evil except this—that God wills goodness. No other motive save that can turn the faces of men towards the heights.

IV

The greatest of all questions then is this—how most efficiently to bring that motive to bear upon the nation. It is in the early and plastic years that the destiny of individuals is fixed. If anywhere, it is in our schools that our children shall learn the things out of which are the issues of life and death. What atmosphere shall we surround our children with in our schools? is the supreme question. 'To educate without religion is only to produce clever devils,' declared the Duke of Wellington in his downright way. And as a nation we have made sure of everything being taught—except religion. No government-inspector ever asks about it!

What a waste it all is and what a travesty—this pumping of facts and figures into the weary, jaded brains of little children. Only five per cent. or so of the people are capable of benefiting by a long process of education—yet everybody must be confined in dreary barracks from five to fifteen years, learning things that will never be of use and are straightway forgotten. We ordained that all the children should be taught, but in our usual blundering fashion we never settled what we should teach them. The child looks out on a world of wonder, and proves its wisdom by peopling every grove and every hill with fairies. For the child the world is spiritual. And it comes to us and asks how came it and why came it? But our legislators decreed that, so far as they were concerned, the child should be taught geography and the names of rivers and hills, but not about the God who made the rivers and hills and the world; botany, but not about the God who made the grass and the flowers; physiology, but not about the God who fashioned man; dates of kings and of battles, but not about the God whose providence is written over all history; about laws, but not about the Source of all law—the divine commands that regulate human action. The only part of man that the educators considered was the brain. If they intellectualised the race they deemed that the millennium would come. They did it. But the millennium is further off than ever. They caused all the people to go through the mills where knowledge was ground out; they learned to read and write. The only consequence was that they became the victims of every charlatan. They turned their arithmetic into roguery and their literature into lust. They became the victims of the gamblers and the betting touts. They pursued the missing words and became the disciples of demagogues. And salvation has tarried though the brain has been nurtured. Yes! there has come a vast progress! London in the next war can be completely destroyed by spraying it with gas bombs—in eight hours! Education, with God left out, will, then, have come to its fruition!

V

National education will only become a means of deliverance from evil when our schools shall have been transformed into the nurseries of goodness. For after all, what we need is good men and women. Clever men are as common as berries; what the world cries for is men who can be trusted, men whose motive will be the welfare of others and not their own. 'His fame was immense,' was the verdict on a Roman patriot; 'his private property was so scanty that there was not enough to pay the expenses of his funeral. He was buried at the public cost. The matrons mourned him as they mourned

Brutus.' Ah! the terrible thing is not to die poor but to die with a character no man honours. To train our children to love and desire goodness is our need. The history of the ages is the proof that goodness cannot flourish apart from religion. And the Bible tells the story of the dealing of God with men—of the evolution of religion. It is that which constitutes the supreme value of the book.

But no book has suffered more at the hands of its friends than has the Bible. The Bible is an Eastern book, and it is filled with glowing metaphors and parables. Dull, unimaginative Western minds said: 'These are literally true, and unless you believe them so you are lost.' The writer of the beautiful book of Jonah wrote a story rebuking the narrow spirit of the Jews, and his book has become the citadel of all the narrow souls who see nothing in it but the whale. Children should be taught that science and religion cannot contradict each other, because they both are revelations of the one God; that the Bible is full of poetry and parables which the writers never meant that any should mistake for treatises; that the slaughter of the Canaanites and the psalms of cursing are no more of the essence of religion, than the Stuart tyranny the essence of Scotland; that the serpent in the garden and Jonah in the whale are parables; that religion, in short, is a flowing and deepening river and not a stagnant pool. But religion as too often taught in our schools is only the teaching of things which the growing boy discovers to be untrue. So far from doing good, it is the destruction of religion.

When the Bible is taught as the record of the evolution of the revelation of God, it will move the hearts of men towards goodness while time endures, for it enshrines the figure of Him who based a Kingdom on love and meekness—a Kingdom that endures for ever, because no guns can fight against a Spirit, nor any frontiers bar it. The education that has not this as its base may produce the chlorine gas—but it will never produce that goodness which alone maketh great. But the course is so crowded that something must be jettisoned. And as inspectors take no note of religion—let it be thrown overboard. Its total omission in Secondary Schools is declared necessary, because the syllabus is too crowded already! It is as if a man having a ship laden with dross were offered some nuggets of fine gold and answered, 'My ship is overloaded already, I cannot take more.' But he wouldn't be such a fool. He would throw everything overboard, if need be, to make room!

VI

In the last year of the Great War a new Education Bill was passed for the Northern Kingdom, and provision was made for everything but the teaching of religion. At every election the voters who desire that religion be continued must have another spell of sentry-go to secure it—all except Roman

Catholics and Episcopalians! Truly we are of the race of the Bourbons. The expense of teaching has been trebled; the futility of what is taught remains as before. I heard the Chairman of an Education Authority being asked whether provision was made in the schools for teaching the children the scientific facts about alcohol. He replied that the syllabus was too crowded already! Alcohol has claimed more victims from humanity than all the wars and famines of all the centuries; and yet our children were not to be taught the truth about it because the syllabus was so crowded! What is it they teach that could compare in value with the truths of temperance and self-discipline? Through a course of training so expensive that the countryside is well-nigh bankrupt because of its cost, the children pass and they go forth into the world unwarned of the rocks and shoals on which the millions have perished.... That, at this time of day, we should shut the doors of our schools against the knowledge of God, in whose love alone men can find their healing, and against the teaching of truth and temperance, which alone can make children grow in character and goodness, seems possible only on the supposition that we have been bereft of our judgment. 'If they do abolish God from their poor bewildered hearts,' said Carlyle, 'all or most of them, there will be seen for some length of time, perhaps for some centuries, such a world as few are dreaming of.'

CHAPTER XI

THERE WERE IN THE SAME COUNTRY SHEPHERDS

'He would denounce the horrors of Christmas until it almost made me blush to look at a hollyberry.'—EDMUND GOSSE'S *Father and Son*.

The world is moving so fast that, before each nightfall, yesterday is forgotten. Sitting here before the fire I have been stirring up my memory, and, out of the subconscious, queer recollections have emerged. I can see now the grim-faced Highland minister demonstrating in the month of December to his perfect satisfaction that the Founder of Christianity was born in midsummer, and that Christmas was but a pagan festival sprinkled over with holy water so-called. I think it was the first time I heard of Christmas. That good man denounced the horrors of Christmas with such zest that I, too, would have blushed to look at a hollyberry—only no holly grew in that part of the Isle. And that was so not because the Isle was remote and the folk spoke there an ancient and little-known language that segregated them from the great life of the world. It was the same in great centres very conscious of their own culture. It was really only yesterday that Walter Smith was dealt with by his presbytery for holding the first Christmas service in his church in Edinburgh. But we have travelled far since that particular yesterday, and I am glad that the children of to-day will never need to blush before a hollyberry. For from the Solway to the Pentland Firth the church bells everywhere to-day summon the people to keep holy day and go on pilgrimage to Bethlehem.

I

There was never a time when the people of this land needed more to go on such a pilgrimage. There are ample signs that Mammon has captured the hearts of this generation. The day is gone on which Ruskin declared that there is no wealth but life. We have outlived that. A full bank account and an empty house—that is our modern wealth. The rich flaunt their riches in a world seething with discontent. And the aforetime quiescent masses now demand that Mammon should smile on them. Society may perish, but they must have their full share in the largesse of Mammon. On the altar of that god duty and patriotism are laid as the meet offering. 'Great is Mammon,' is the burden of the praise of our day. And what a god before whom to bow the knee!

It is only when I go on pilgrimage to-day to the grotto in the rock in which the asses were stabled in Bethlehem and to the stall where the Child is laid that I can realise the vulgarity and the meanness of Mammon. Out of that manger there issued a power compared to which all other influences that moulded men are as the rushlight to the sun; in that stable lies the fountain out of which sprang the river that has borne on its bosom for nineteen centuries all of beauty and of truth and of love wherewith humanity has been blessed; and yet all that came out of the direst poverty. Mammon had no smile for the greatest and most radiant thing in all the world's history. Money secures at least food and shelter, and it was because they had none that the innkeeper shut them out. If they could have showed him a purse full of gold pieces, he would soon have made room. And all the life of this Jesus was woven after that pattern. The cheapest food sold then were sparrows. It was because He was often sent to buy them that He knew that two of them were sold in the market place for a farthing. The patched garment is the symbol of poverty—or used to be! And He knew all about garments being patched and patched until they were past mending. At the eventide when the boy James brought a coat to be mended He heard His mother say with a weary sigh: 'I have mended this again and again: nobody can keep boys in decent clothes; so different from girls; a new patch will just tear a bigger hole in the old.' Often He saw His mother cast a half-farthing into the treasury, for she had nought else. The tax-gatherer comes, and there isn't a coin to pay. Jesus gave much, but He never gave any money, for He had none to give. He was homeless for three years, deemed mad by His family, with no place where to lay His head. A grave given in charity receives Him at the last. The place of Jesus from the manger to the grave is among the poorest of the poor. He belonged to the great class of the disinherited. If the greatest thing on earth sprang from poverty such as this, then surely Christmas pours the contempt of heaven upon Mammon.

II

We have only to look at him with eyes cleansed by gazing at the Child in the manger and we realise how tawdry a god this Mammon is. What can he do for us? Nothing of any worth. He has never minted a coinage which can buy the inspiration of a noble thought, which can purchase love for the starved heart, or can endow a man with the vision and the faculty divine. One has but to consider a moment and he will realise the poverty-stricken condition of Mammon's devotees. They can command speed on earth or in the air; they can fly a hundred miles an hour; but what is the good when at the end of the hundred miles they are as at the beginning—sated, restless, and dissatisfied? They can command no speed by which they can escape from themselves. And it is vain to wing a flight upwards through the air if heaven be empty overhead; vain to alight five hundred miles away if on earth there be no temple, no holy day, no shrine at which to worship. 'You own the land,' said the poor painter to the new-rich who boasted his land: 'you own the land but

I own the landscape.' The great gift is to own the landscape. And no money ever bought that. The only thing Mammon can do is to secure food, shelter, and clothes. It can also secure freedom from work—but that is a freedom shared with the tramp. Life is greater far than livelihood; and the worshippers of Mammon lose the very essence and the end of life in a vain pursuit of the means of living.

That is the witness raised by Christmas as it calls the nations to realise the true greatness of man. To a generation that has made life a hectic rush after money and pleasure, Christmas testifies that to estimate any man by the money he owns is to blaspheme against the Child laid in the manger. The wealth of Croesus makes him but the prey of the conqueror, and the dust of centuries has buried the pomp and glory of emperors. But this Child, cradled in poverty, reigns from generation to generation. The voice of an Alexander or a Napoleon would to-day cause no heart to beat quicker; but millions would die for Him. And that because He alone revealed to men the things that are unpurchasable, the riches that are unseen. He alone made men realise that a man's life consisteth not in the things that he possesseth, but rather in the thoughts that he thinks, in the motives that sway his action; in the ideals towards which he presses; in the God whom he worships and makes his own. How great a revolution He made. That one hour in the manger has changed the world. Every time I sit down to write a letter and head it 1922 I bear witness to the truth—that the world I know began when a Child laid in the manger brought to earth the realisation that all the great and noble things in life can be mine—though my raiment be shabby and though my banker never thinks it worth his while to throw me even a word when I reluctantly pass in through his swing door. What a wonderful new wine He brought, and how generously does He pour it into our bottles. Still new—after nineteen centuries! Still bursting the old bottles on all sides! I can be quite patient. There is no need for passionately tearing them in pieces. Nineteen centuries! What are they in the arithmetic of eternity! Give the Child time—and all the bottles of Mammon and vulgarity will at last be burst.

III

No wonder Christmas sends a glow of warmth round the heart, and causes joy bells to ring in the souls of even the drooping. It is to-day as it was of old, when the disciples—poor, dull, purblind men—were disputing even near the end as to which of them would have the greater position and the greater wealth and honour. And Jesus placed a little child in the midst and said, 'Except ye be converted, and become as a little child, ye cannot enter the kingdom.' And in a world weary of disputing, sated with strife as to who is to have the higher place and the greater portion, Christmas places the Child in the midst and says, 'Except ye be converted...' What men need is not the sharing of a booty, but the regenerating of a Spirit. The faith, the trust, the purity, the love of the childlike spirit—that's what we need. What we do or what we get matters nought, if only that spirit be in the heart. One man may whirl past in a Rolls-Royce, befurred, bejewelled, and may be the most pauperised soul on earth; while the stone-breaker at the roadside may be the inheritor of all things and rich beyond all dreams. Christmas is the surety of that. That was the wisdom of 'Stonecracker John,' who sang:—

'The good Lord made the earth and sky,
The river and the sea—and me!
He made no roads, but here am I
As happy as can be;
For it is just as if he said—
"John, that's the job for thee."
And so in my appointed place,
By God's good grace,
I work, according to his plan,
And would not change with any man.'

To-day, as it has done for the centuries and the years that are so many that one wearies in counting them, Christmas throws the halo of beauty over all shepherds abiding in the fields calling on their dogs; over all toilers in mines and workshops; over all stonebreakers and street-sweepers; over all mothers and all babes. It proclaims to-day with a voice whose certainty changes not that the man who serves Mammon and gains the world while he loses his soul makes a grievous and a profitless barter.

CHAPTER XII

THE FULNESS OF THE TIME

If there be no will guiding the affairs of men towards a predestined end, what a meaningless welter it all is! What a record of wars and feuds, of rising and of perishing empires, of civilisations born and civilisations overwhelmed: in very truth

'A tale
Told by an idiot: full of sound and fury
Signifying nothing.'

There is unity and a new dignity in the tale when one gets up on a hill and sees it in far perspective. Things did not happen by chance. There was through it all a purpose at work, welding humanity together with the cement of blood, throwing down the barriers of race and language, silencing the sound of tumult and war until at last the song is heard on the plain of Bethlehem that has sung itself into the hearts of men, ushering in the dawn of peace and goodwill. In the fulness of the time the Child was laid in the manger.

I

Every advance of humanity in its upward struggle has sprung from some divine dissatisfaction. It was the fulness of the time in that the world, disillusioned and dissatisfied, realised its need. The Greek found no answer for their moral needs in the pantheon of gods that filled the heart with the passion for beauty alone. Socrates before drinking the hemlock advised his disciples to search for another teacher; but that other could not be found. The only remedy for the ills of man that they discovered was that he should cut himself loose from the world—a gospel of suicide. The Roman made a god of power. But when he had conquered the world, invested it with roads and bridges and by force had imposed peace on it, then he confronted the awful mystery of his own personality, and his questioning was baffled by a silence in which there was no voice nor any that answered. His gods became objects of derision. In the gratification of his bodily cravings he sought to lull the hunger of his soul. At last Rome presented the dread spectacle of a Nero who was at once 'a priest, an atheist, and a god.' There is preserved a record which visualises the awful depths to which that pagan world descended. Nero had murdered his mother, and he comes back to Rome nervous as to how the people will receive him. But the citizens poured out to meet him in their thousands, and rent the welkin with their shouts of welcome—'Hail, Nero, the god!' If that world was to be saved, it had to be saved then. If God was ever to intervene in the affairs of men, He had to intervene then. The extremity of man was God's opportunity. The Unseen Ruler must either come and deliver a world such as that or abdicate. The coming of the Child was a necessity.

II

It is very hard to understand how things do happen; and our only comfort is that we really understand nothing. We have in these last years been mesmerised into thinking that we understand a great deal when in reality we understand nothing at all. We camouflage our ignorance by speaking of law—but what is it? Why do like causes produce a like result always? No answer. We used to explain the heavens by gravitation. What is it? No answer. We ushered in the new age of electricity. What is it! Silence! There is no reason, then, for rebelling against the fact that we cannot understand the greatest of all mysteries—the coming of God more fully into the lives of men. All we can hope to do is to realise how natural it is that God should so come to men. As the years pass that thought becomes more and more natural. In other days God was thought of as dwelling far removed from the world. That is not now the great thought regarding God. 'Whatever sort of being God may be,' writes William James, 'He is nevermore that mere external inventor of contrivances intended to manifest His glory in which our great-grandfathers took such satisfaction.' (The conception of our great-grandfathers may have been limited; but it is more important that we should try to be as good men as they were.) This conception of 'an absentee God outside the world watching it go,' has given place to another. The world is now realised as spiritual through and through; the shrine of an indwelling life. God is in the world, has always been in the world, and man's reasoning and loving is but a reflection of his Maker's reason and love. Through all the weary centuries God has been with men, in men, striving with their spirits, never absent from them, the source of all their aspirations, visions, and dreams. If that be so, it is the most natural thing in all history that in the fulness of the time, when the need was greatest, God should come in fuller measure into the lives that He had made. Surely natural that the glows and flashes preceding the dawn should at last break forth into the glory of the sunrise. God, who has been with man from the dawn, guiding and leading, at last in the noontide speaks with the articulate Word, making His purpose clear. If once we realise that there has never been an impassable chasm between God and man, then the incredible becomes credible. For this is not an isolated event; it is rather the beginning of another great stage in man's spiritual evolution by which God comes and dwells more and more in the hearts of men, becoming incarnate in lives risen from the dead; in souls renewed after His image.

III

With us, too, it is the fulness of the time. If God intervenes when the need is sorest, and when man realises the need—then we can well cherish the expectation that another manifestation of God is at hand. Nineteen centuries ago He came to a world whose religion was dead. With us it is not dead; it is sore stricken. The glow has vanished, and those who bow down in the house of God in our day do so largely from force of habit, and not because they believe. Religion to-day curbs few evils, and is powerless against the selfishness that sacrifices the well-being of nations on the altars of self-interest. And, just as in Rome the unrest of soul made the degenerate a prey to every charlatan and soothsayer that came out of the East, so the spiritual hunger of our day brings men and women to crystal-gazers and table-rappers, bowing down before every superstition, however gross. And if the Rome of the Cæsars sought to allay its soul hunger at the banquets of pleasure, so also with us. Low forms of pleasure have led the multitudes captive. The London of Charles II. could not hold a candle to the London or Glasgow of to-day in the way of refinements of material sensation. The old cry of 'bread and circuses' has given place to the cry of dancing-halls and doles! In that old world at last there was no room for the cradle in the family life—the babe was shut out. And so to-day. There is every sign that God must again intervene and save, or the civilisation we know will be buried with the civilisations of all the past. The fountain of inspiration, of cleansing, of righteousness must be opened afresh, and its reviving waters sent flowing over all the land. Unless God does so come there is no hope. But all history is the proof that He will so come. We can hear the rumble of His chariot wheels as He comes. Here and there the Spirit is moving on the face of the waters. Of old it was shepherds and fishermen who first received the glad tidings. That fishermen should be the first to feel the coming outrush of spiritual power in our day is wholly natural. The glad tidings of Christmas is that God is ever coming to His own. The duty laid upon us is that we prepare His way, and make room for Him. It will be a new Edinburgh and a new Glasgow when the renewing Spirit shall have swept through them. It is the one hope. In Melrose Abbey there is an old inscription, 'When Jesus comes the shadows depart.' Some monk who felt the shadows gathering round him realised Christ as a living presence—and the shadows were wafted away. And he carved the words. And our shadows will vanish when He who lay in the manger will come again, in the fulness of His reviving and quickening Spirit. Then God will again work marvels in transfigured lives and in nations reborn.

IV

There are some good people to whom the word Revival is anathema. There have always been such people. 'Their doctrines are most repulsive, and strongly tinctured with impertinence and disrespect to their superiors,' wrote the Duchess of Buckingham to Lady Huntingdon, regarding the early Methodists. 'It is monstrous to be told that you have a heart as sinful as the common wretches that crawl the earth. This is highly insulting, and I wonder that your Ladyship should relish any sentiment so much at variance with high rank and good breeding.' Yet it was that same Revival of religion in the days of Wesley and Whitefield that saved England when the evil days befell in the end of the eighteenth century and the beginning of the nineteenth. There is no nobler figure in all history than that of John Wesley riding over the whole country, reading as he rode, contesting all England for God, everywhere wakening the dead. To duchesses and highly refined folk that Revival seemed to be 'repulsive' and 'monstrous.' Religion was good enough in its own place, but it must not interfere with their amusements. They wanted their religion well iced. To-day when only another such outrush of spiritual energy can save a poor sick world, there is no need to trouble about the mocker. There is only reason to rejoice that there are manifest stirrings in the depths of human life which no earthly theory can explain. Often and often on wearied men there comes the breath of a new life, and armies, long worn out, arise and snatch redemption out of ruin. The prelude to these triumphs of the Spirit has always been a sense of expectation springing up mysteriously out of the depths. That expectation is wholly natural. We have come through the most awful carnival of blood and tears in the world's history, and so far there has been no result commensurate with the sacrifice. The old world is dead and the new tarries while men are left

'Wandering between two worlds, one dead,
The other powerless to be born,'

If man's extremity be God's opportunity, then, once more, it is the fulness of the time.

CHAPTER XIII

VICTORY OUT OF RUIN

The world has always been a hard place for minorities. Majorities are capable of crimes which, as individuals, they would shrink from in horror. And no crimes that stain the pages of history can equal in ghastly cruelty those which have been perpetrated under the influence of religious passions. The Founder of Christianity was crucified at the frenzied call of those who were the most devout and religious of their day. The Pharisees prayed nine hours a day! Their cry, 'Crucify! Crucify!' still rings in the ear.

I

Human nature has not changed very much in these nineteen centuries. And the majority of mankind are still pretty much as they were. There is not much good in getting suffused with sentiment over a minority of one crucified so long ago. It is more important to realise that the grim tragedy is for ever and for ever being repeated. It is a grim thought to think that the very passions of self-righteousness and self-interest which crucified the Galilean are now operating in His name. In a little village in the Hebrides well known to me, four Presbyterian churches celebrate the Communion in August. Here they are—the Parish Church; the United Free Church; the Free Church; the Free Presbyterian Church! If you attended a service in any of these you would not know any difference between them. On all vital matters they are at one. But there they are in the very name of Christ negating His purpose and breaking His law. For His purpose is to unite men together; bring them into the fellowship and unity of love. And they break up that small community into four fragments—and they do it from the highest motives and under the sanctions of the name of the Highest. They act exactly as the Pharisees acted nineteen centuries ago. They too were moved by the highest motives; they too had a passion for the Sabbath. The Christians to-day, like the Pharisee of old, make the gospel vain by their traditions. If He came Himself and said to them, 'You are wrong: my law is that ye love one another: the sign of my faithful followers is the love their lives evince,' ... He wouldn't be listened to. They would not cry 'Crucify.' ... No! They would only give Him a nickname and declare that He had no right principles! ... But it isn't in remote villages one beholds that. It can be seen anywhere. Moderators and bishops and dignitaries have met for a quarter of a century in Edinburgh to knock at the door of heaven with petitions asking God to unite them! And they will meet anywhere—in licensed premises even—except in a church; they will do anything except have the Communion together.... And they go on praying!

To-day the very bigotry that sent the Lord stumbling to Calvary under a Cross is glorified by the name of Christ. That to-day is His crucifixion.

II

That, however, is but half a truth. When we take long views we can realise that there is no day in the year when we have more right to cherish the spirit of hope than on this day when the world waits for the Easter joy bells: Rejoice, Rejoice. The message of a day such as this is that no cause that has in it the seed of righteousness, however feeble it may be and however overwhelming its opponents, need give way to despair. There never was a minority so feeble on the face of the earth as these Galileans whose Master had been crucified. The cause was lost. They had not even understood what He had tried to teach them. While He spoke of a kingdom not of this world they could think of nothing but pitiful thrones such as Herod's! They left Him in a minority of one—and that minority was crucified. Nobody in all the wide world knew or understood why He hung there.... He who was to smash the Gentiles, as the Jew believed, was there crucified by Gentiles; He who was innocent was stamped for ever with the criminal's brand—done to death with two thieves. If ever there was an end made of any cause there was an end made of that personified by the Carpenter of Nazareth. The majority trampled the minority into extinction.

The body can be crucified and can be sealed up in a tomb, but majorities are powerless against the spirit. When his disciples asked Socrates where they would bury him he replied: 'You can bury me anywhere if you can catch me!' The soul can never be caught; can never be sealed up in a tomb. The wind bloweth where it listeth; and no walls, however high, can imprison it; no tomb hold it. Out of the dust the new life arose—the life of the spirit. And suddenly men realised that a kingdom not of this world—an empire without legions—was not only thinkable and possible, but was actually established. So has it always been since: the perishing of the body has been but the triumphing of the spirit.

III

One of the miracles of history is the way in which that crucified ideal arose and conquered; in which peasants and fishermen went forth to sow the seed of an invisible kingdom beneath the feet of militarists and tyrants, who though they rooted it up could never destroy it, until at last the minority was transformed into a majority. And that same miracle is for ever being repeated. What happened then happens now. And there are two reasons for that. The first is that man is much nobler than he is himself aware of. Beneath the subliminal consciousness there are untold riches—golden ore waiting to be mined. Under the influence of the herd-instinct and of crowd-psychology a man can on Friday yell, Crucify! Crucify! but on Saturday he may enter the valley of repentance and be made anew. Memory awakes in him when he is alone. He recalls the face and the words of the Crucified; doubts arise as to whether it was right—that cry of Crucify. No malefactor could have borne himself like that.... Long-forgotten feelings are let loose. Truly that Man had a regal spirit. However much a man may sink, he never sinks below the capacity of feeling the contagion of a triumphant spirit. Where is the man who cannot thrill as he hears Livingstone say, 'I'll go anywhere, provided it is forward'? It is in that hidden depth the hope of humanity lies. The cause that seems lost rallies to its side the multitudes that no sooner do the wrong than they are smitten with shame therefor and repent thereof. From the ranks of its enemies the cause of righteousness ever recruits its most valiant fighters. The Sauls are transformed into Pauls, and powerless minorities into triumphing majorities.

Not only are the laws of the spirit on the side of the righteous minority, but also the laws of the universe. The cause of reform cannot ultimately be defeated because the unchanging laws of nature are arrayed against evil. The great ally of every righteous minority is death. That was how Christianity conquered at the first. The Christians lived righteous lives, and by the very laws of life outlived the Pagans. So is it now. The life of self-indulgence and self-interest has no vitality to resist. Death removes it. The ranks of the devotees of pleasure are being swiftly depleted. Death is the great ally of righteousness. The multitude, who wanted to turn back to Egypt, 'died by the plague before the Lord' in the wilderness. Some virulent influenza came—and they hadn't the stamina to resist! ... That's how majorities vanish and room is made for the vigorous and healthy minority to possess the land.

IV

The Calvaries of Christ are to-day everywhere. Wherever a child hungers or perishes, wherever men and women decay and die, there He, who identifies Himself with men, is again crucified. Where little babies die, 200 out of every thousand; where in proportion to the number of licensed premises is the death-rate among the babes—there He is crucified. Here, in this capital city, an hour in the evening has been added to the hours on which the monopolists in alcohol prey on the people, that more homes may be ruined and more children perish. It seems utterly hopeless. What is the use of trying to arouse people so dead to the decencies of life as this? But, to-morrow, the city will begin to be ashamed. The Church will begin to rouse itself. When Lord Shaftesbury was toiling to free 35,000 children from five to thirteen years in Lancashire alone from the Moloch of the factory he wrote—'The sinners are with me and the saints against me.' That is indeed weird: how often has the Church looked on, indifferent, while wrong triumphed. There is nothing more pathetic than to see the Church mustering up courage to condemn what the world has already judged and set aside! ... But to-day the message that comes across all the centuries to the heart of all minorities struggling for the right is this—'Be of good cheer: victory is on the way: though it tarry, wait for it!' The darkness of Calvary is but the prelude to the triumph of Easter morning.

Milton Keynes UK
Ingram Content Group UK Ltd.
UKHW030913151124
451262UK00006B/781